British Lorries 1900~1945

British Lorries 1900~1945

C. F. Klapper

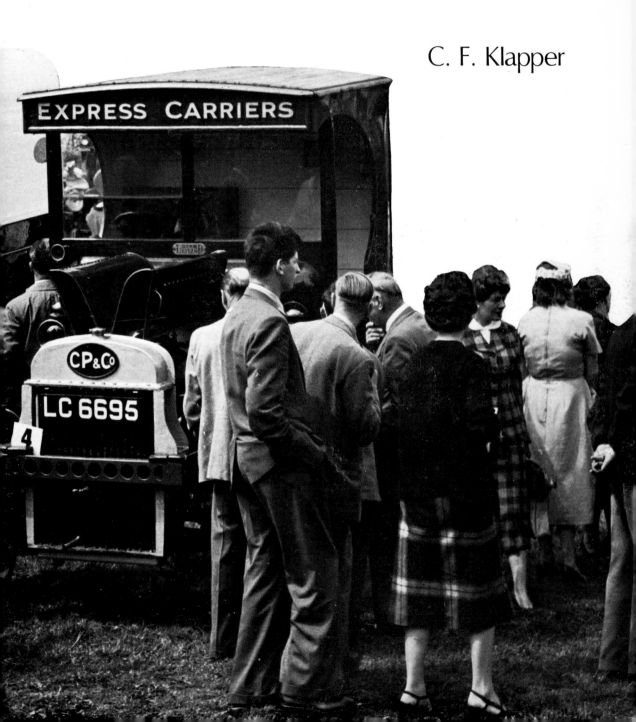

First Published 1973

ISBN 0 7110 0455 2

Ian Allan Ltd. 1973

Printed and Published by
Ian Allan Ltd, Shepperton, TW17 8AS

Contents

Introduction

Much the most significant transport change of the century to the man and woman in the street has been the rise of motor transport. Everyone knows about the motor car and how it has changed the lives of all of us. We all use the bus, if only when our personal transport is being serviced. But unobtrusively the motor lorry, the mechanised road freight vehicle, has made itself the servant of us all. From hesitant beginnings it gathered strength and power; it became swifter and stronger and, greatly daring, took over work from the horse, that noble animal so beloved by the English that they let it work itself to death before their very eyes.

Stimulated by the tasks of war the motor lorry emerged in 1919 ready to do battle with the established means of long-distance movement, the railway. Despite cries of co-ordination over the years, it has undertaken in its persuasive sweep forward the conveyance of everything from the smallest package to the largest indivisible loads that can be moved by any means of transport. Road haulage now carries more than four-fifths of the originating tonnage of the goods shifted from one place to another in these islands to provide our food, our amenities, our work and the exports by which we live.

On the way to becoming a maid-of-all-work to the community the lorry has become refined technically; the steamer thundering on steel tyres was only excelled as a noise producer by the pickaxe blows on the granite setts of the day of the horse teams it superseded; as the petrol engine grew more powerful it acquired almost absolute silence; its gearbox ceased to moan and the tread of the vehicle was hushed, first by solid rubber, then by cushion and finally by the giant pneumatic tyre. If the more efficient diesel engine has caused some setback in noise emission one can reflect that the level of polution it creates is considerably reduced. Very slowly, with strict regulation and anxious inquiry by the Ministries concerned before each upward step, the dimensions of lorries have grown, although we have a severe weight (and therefore load) limitation unknown to most of our trade rivals on the Continent of Europe, despite their encouragement of railway and canal facilities. Perhaps, in view of the amenities the road vehicle brings to modern life, this matter should be looked upon rather from the viewpoint of enlargement of through highways than from that of blanket restriction on the vehicles.

The changes from the early days of the commercial vehicle to the present are, despite restriction, most remarkable; in a working life of nearly 50 years in transport the author has seen it all, from the haulage office where he started, full of curry combs and chaff dust, with the yard outside only occasionally desecrated by the odour of petrol, but from which the manure was an extremely marketable by-product, to the sophisticated motor vehicle depots where super haulage business is conducted today, aided by washing machines, precision maintenance equipment, container lifting gear and other freight handling plant, plus computers for delivery round calculations, documentation and accounting.

The technical development of the motor vehicle for haulage work is a fascinating story which can be read in part at the Science Museum and to a degree at the National Motor Museum, taken over in the summer of 1972 from Lord Montagu of Beaulieu's remarkable collection of motors. Alas, simple considerations of space restrict the number of commercials to 16, and excellent though the specimens preserved there may be, the story can be told only sketchily. It is supplemented, of course, by the large number of historic lorries and vans restored by loving and enthusiastic private hands; they are preserved with the aid of the Historic Commercial Vehicle Club and other such bodies.

Some of the gaps in a long story of empiric improvement and diversity of aim are filled by this album of photographs from the files of *Modern Transport*. They may serve to remind the reader of

Mechanical traction on the roads of Britain owes a good deal to the pioneers of steam vehicles who kept the road motor vehicle a going concern, despite its powerful opponents and detractors, throughout the Victorian era. This is the Grenville steamer of 1875, which figured in the Regents Park jubilee cavalcade organised by the Society of Motor Manufacturers & Traders in 1946 and suffered throughout the first 21 years of its existence a speed limited to walking pace. *Fox Photos*

Road freight transport before the 1900's is typified by this horse-drawn furniture van bought by Heaton of St Helens in 1899 . . .

.... and by contrast one of the Heaton successor company's tractor and semi-trailer outfits of 1967. Studio Argent.

An original type of steamer was the Yorkshire; this one, seen at Horsham Historic Vehicle Show in 1970, was built in 1914 by Yorkshire Patent Steam Wagon Co Ltd, of Hunslet, Leeds. The double-ended boiler, placed transversely on the frame, did well on coke fuel because the flues were comparatively short; the water level was not adversely affected by steep gradients. S. W. Stevens-Stratten

One of many electrics, that, despite prejudice among users against their short radius of action, have rendered good service on local delivery work. This is a restored Walker vehicle. American built and owned from 1919-1930 by Chloride Electrical Storage Corpn, and now preserved by Harrods. S. W. Stevens-Stratten

many of the splendid machines which after the emancipation of 1896, played their part between 1900 and 1945 in building up the economy of modern Britain.

Let it also be a tribute to the sturdy pioneering work of colleagues in road haulage and own-account transport and to the vehicle manufacturers, without whose faith in the product, venturing of capital, devoted research and hard-slogging salesmanship we should not have had a road haulage industry of today's competence; moreover, without the same highly efficient road transport at home the country would have been the poorer for lack of the export business achieved by the excellence of the British commercial vehicle.

A book such as this owes much to the enthusiasm and ready assistance of many people. In particular I acknowledge the help of E. L. Cornwell, who was in charge of *Modern Transport* road tests from 1954 to 1968; S. W. Stevens-Stratten, Editor of *Model Railway Constructor* , whose collection of rally photographs has been drawn upon to illustrate a number of vehicles which have escaped preservation in the files; and T. H. Everitt, veteran photographer of vehicles under test, who worked on behalf of *Modern Transport* in the 1930's.

One final word to do-it-yourself vehicle testers: Succombs Hill has a severe weight restriction today and Miry Miriam and Crown Ash Hill are both closed to motor vehicles.

AEC

The AEC marque of vehicle had a mysterious birth in the overhaul works of the Vanguard bus undertaking at Walthamstow (hence the telegraphic address "Vangastow," even though the factory has been at Southall for four decades). Vanguard merged in London General and after the Underground group's takeover of the bus company the Associated Equipment Co Ltd was formed to hive off and expand the manufacturing business. The first AEC lorries were on B type bus chassis adapted as garage lorries by the LGOC; came the 1914 war and AEC was pitched into large-scale freight-carrier manufacture with the aid of Daimler of Coventry and Tyler the engine builder. Some of these survive and can be seen at Historic Commercial Vehicle rallies. The first AEC designed as a commercial was the 2-tonner of 1924, the lightest and smallest AEC ever produced. The true lines of the present freight vehicles emerged after the transfer to Southall in 1927, with the energetic introduction of the diesel, after much pioneer effort and testing of the market at the end of the 'twenties and the adoption of refined components in the Regal and Regent bus range which were matched to the lorries of the Monarch, Matador and Mammoth series in the thirties. The Mammoth Major eight-wheeler was the first rigid eight-wheeler for civilian use and prototypes operated during 1933. Production in earnest was announced in 1934. Maximum gross weight was 22ton and a payload of 15ton was possible, plus or minus a little according to whether the 120bhp petrol or 130 bhp diesel engine was fitted. Today AEC is part of the British Leyland group.

Opposite: A Monarch built in 1937; it ran 16 000 miles in 1938 at a cost of 22½p for electric bulbs and 37½p for repairs while delivering Royal Irish linen thread in Northern Ireland

Smallest and lightest of the AEC freight vehicles was the 2-ton model of 1924; it had a 24.7hp (RAC rating) four-cylinder petrol engine.

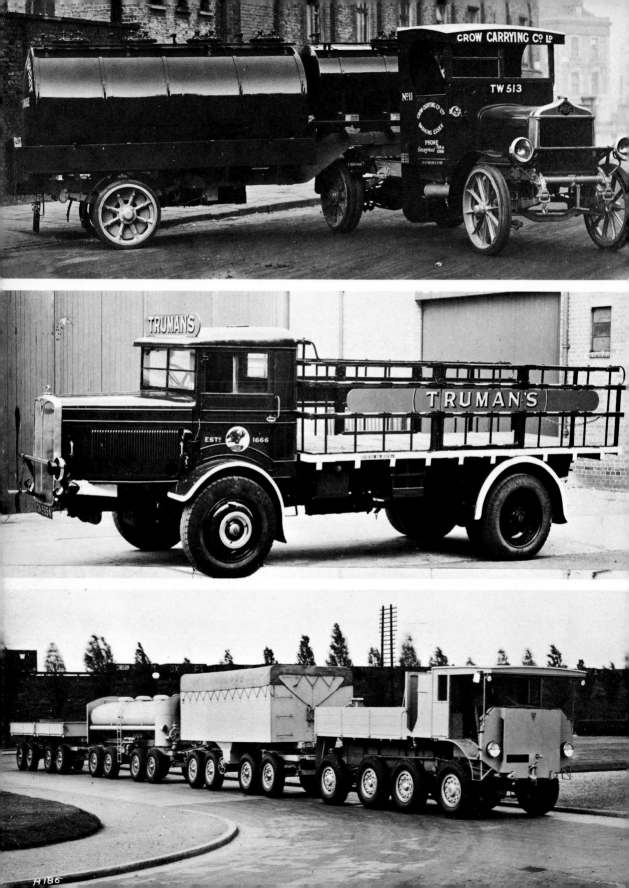

Top left: An articulated made from a four-wheeler in 1926

Centre: A snout-bonneted Majestic rebuilt at nine years old for further service in 1940

Bottom left: A 1935 rigid eight-wheeler designed for special trailer haulage in Russia

Above: A splendid space for advertisement display was provided on the side of this Mammoth Major Eight van built in 1934

Below: The modern rally fashion with parades of restored vehicles; Northampton Brewery's Tyler-engined AEC 3-4 tonner of 1919

Albion

Only remaining vehicle of purely Scottish origin was Albion. Gone are the valiant ghosts of the past — Arrol-Johnston, Beardmore, Caledon, Halley, the privately-built Lothian (a bus for the Scottish Motor Traction group) — but first under the Leyland banner and then as part of the British Leyland Motor Corporation group the Albion flag flew till 1972 at Scotstoun, prouder than ever. The Albion management under the new regime looks after the former British Motor Corporation factory at Bathgate. The year after the Albion Motor Car Co Ltd began business in 1901 its commercial vehicles began to be used for the deliveries of highly respected household-name products. There was a built-in ruggedness in Albions — which came out in the "sure as the sunrise" slogan and in turn gave rise to the design on the radiator header — and an adherence to well-tried principles which endeared them to their owners. Chain-drive persisted through thousands of subsidy type lorries turned out for the War Department in the 1914 upheaval. In the thirties the chairman of the company denounced the diesel engine — but his technical staff made a first-class diesel to satisfy the customers. Type designations inclined to be unwieldy combinations of letters, figures and tonnages, but eventually the general practice of handy type names, represented recently by Chieftain, Reiver and similar designations, prevailed.

Service to a growing circle of customers, with adequate supplies of spares and know-how, was an Albion feature and by the end of the thirties Albion chassis were well in the van for excellence of design and modern appearance. Today the vehicles are known as "Leyland Glasgow."

Opposite: By 1922 pneumatic tyres had appeared on light lorries; these three of the McVitie & Price fleet shared the carrying of wedding cake for Princess Mary, the Princess Royal, upon her marriage to Lord Harewood in February of that year.

Right: The famous Albion 3-tonner, eligible for War Office subsidy before 1914, retained chain drive and performed yeoman service for the Army in the 1914-18 war. Built in 1918 this one — top speed 13mph — was spruced up for the 1971 Trans-Pennine rally.
S. W. Stevens-Stratten.

Below: Albion commercial vehicles began to be built as long ago as 1902 when tiller steering was still fashionable. This very first 10cwt van, Model A2, had a 7hp engine.

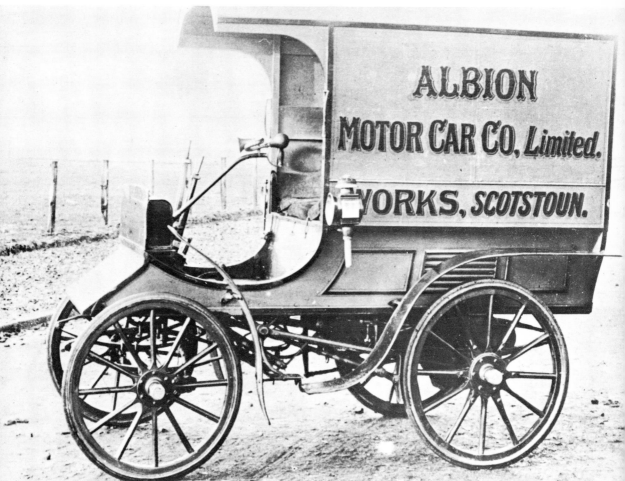

Above: The A14 15cwt 15hp lorry which was built until 1915. This one is in the Montagu collection, now the National Motor Museum, founded by Lord Montagu of Beaulieu.

Right: Chain drive had disappeared from the A16 20hp 20cwt van, built in 1919-20.

Far right: A 2½-tonner crosses the Miry Mirian watersplash on the Modern Transport test route for commercial vehicles in 1930. T. H. Everitt.

18

Above: The 5ton overtype on meat haulage from London's Smithfield Market in 1931

Top right: An Albion oil-engined export model with semi-trailer collects a 20ton load from the quayside in Sydney, New South Wales, during the 1939-45 war.

Right: By 1939 the Albion 15ton eight-wheeler with EN 242 engine was in production. The Kirkness Innes bodywork brought the unladen weight to 6ton 13cwt 3qr.

Armstrong-Saurer

Back in 1907 Pickfords bought a large batch of Saurer lorries from Switzerland because of their excellence. It is a connection which was sustained later both vehicle-wise and personally, since the recent head of the Pickford business under the National Freight Corporation regime, Mr Harold Elliott, served his engineering apprenticeship at the Arbon works. At the end of the 1920's it was decided that an English-built version of the Saurer should be put on the British market and the Armstrong-Whitworth group took up the project. Armstrong-Saurer exhibits first appeared at a Commercial Motor Transport Exhibition in 1931. The range was reminiscent of its Swiss ancestry and was in what was then deemed the "heavy" class — the six-wheeled Dominant, with its demonstrably flexible rear bogie, was a 12-tonner. But the English bogie was of pressed steel and not an assembly of massive steel castings, as was its Swiss counterpart. This helped bring the vehicle inside UK weight restrictions. From the outset it was intended to build the entire job at Scotswood-on-Tyne, alongside the Armstrong Whitworth works, but with some production also in Paris this was an early example of internationalism in vehicle building, later to be exploited to the full by the Ford organisation. Advanced features of this 90hp oil-engined job included air brakes and overdrive. Other models were the four-wheeled Dauntless and a four-ton four-wheeled goods model, the Diligent. The Samson rigid eight-wheeled model of 1935 carried tank wagons of up to 22ton all-up weight and was claimed as the largest lorry in the world on its appearance. After the war many an Armstrong-Saurer, retired from haulage, lived a fresh life as a showman's vehicle.

Opposite: Armstrong-Saurer had a good eye for publicity and on July 19th, 1932 a new model diesel-engined six-wheeler was the first vehicle to cross the new Lambeth Bridge from west to east. Another Armstrong-Saurer with a Dyson trailer was in the van of the opposite traffic flow.

Below: The four-wheel steering rigid eight-wheeler just avoids being bogged down in the ruts of the "colonial" section of the Modern Transport Kent and Surrey border test route in 1935.

Bottom: In 1935 this Armstrong-Saurer tanker, with an all-up weight of 22ton and a capacity of 3,300 gallons, was claimed as the world's largest lorry; it is seen alongside the Rytecraft Scooter Truck, the world's smallest, then being launched.

Atkinson

Fate seems to have determined that Edward Atkinson should have to do with transport, although he was trained as a millwright and set up on his own as such. But his first Preston employer was concerned with Horace Viney's early contribution to internal-combustion-engined van design, the front-wheel-drive Pullcar. Then when he set up on his own in 1907 he chose premises close to what is now the A6 main road and found his activities diverted to vehicle repair. Soon he acquired a reputation for being knowledgeable and competent on keeping steam wagons going and in so doing he developed some sound ideas of what would make a good wagon. By a natural process — although at a difficult time in the middle of a war — he designed and built his own, No 1 appearing in January 1916. By 1922 three wagons a week were being turned out and 150 men were on the payroll. At that time Stumpf type uniflow engines were being used and a solitary (uneconomic) 2½ -tonner had mechanical stoking. Despite a short association on steam wagons and locomotives with Walker Bros of Wigan, the depression of the 1920's and disenchantment with steam brought the receivers in. Eventually the reconstructed company attracted the attention of W. G. Allen, of the Nightingale Garage, Clapham, and a fresh start was made in 1933. By 1935, using the reliability and long-life characteristics of the Gardner oil engine, the company had got into its stride again with the modern diesel-engined multi-wheeled pneumatic lorry. If for the first years it still built in smallish numbers it gained enthusiastic adherents among vehicle users by the company's individual attention to their requirements. This close following of specialist needs continues to delight operators of Atkinsons in what has become a well-spread overseas, as well as home, market for Atkinson Vehicles Ltd.

Opposite: In the 1933 reconstruction steam was abandoned for Gardner diesel power and a workmanlike heavy-duty lorry was the result.

Below: In the prime of the reign of the steam wagon on Britain's roads, this Atkinson 6-tonner of a Birmingham area contractor served the thirsty by distributing Worthington.

A six-wheeled tanker on an Atkinson chassis.

An eight-wheeled 15-tonner delivered in 1938; the ringed A on the radiator is complemented by the words "Atkinson" and "Diesel" cast into the frame of the stoneguard. The haulier owner of the vehicle was well-known in the iron and steel trades before nationalisation.

Austin

When young Herbert Austin worked for the Wolseley Tool & Motor Car Company and patented a sheep-shearing machine he had dreams of building his own brand of motor vehicles; in fact, soon after he began car production he was in commercial vehicle manufacture with a 14hp 15cwt delivery van. It was not until 1913 that he achieved a 3-tonner and then it was of pleasingly original design. A four-cylinder engine, with individual cylinder pots bolted on a cast-aluminium crankcase, developed 29bhp at 1,500rpm and was concealed under a cheese-dish bonnet behind which the radiator was mounted. The well-raked steering column came down the bonnet side. Most original feature was the divided drive; the differential was behind the gearbox and twin propeller shafts took the drive through bevels at each end to the live stubs at the ends of the solid drawn steel tube axle. Each drive shaft passed through the centre of a lattice-girder frame. A considerable number of these interesting vehicles were built during the 1914-18 war

and were used on special duties from searchlight vehicles to workshops; in 1919 it was uprated as a 3½-tonner — but selling original designs at that time had powerful competition in the cheap ex-WD units from military dumps. Austin commercials were orthodox for a few years and from 1925 to 1939 went off the public market altogether although the keenness of Lord Austin (as he had become) and his engineers remained unabated and many types were purchased or specially built for works use, so that a good deal of inside knowledge was accumulated. As a result, when it was decided to cut into the commercial vehicle market again it was the light mass-production sector that was chosen and the Austin's resemblance to a successful model from Luton earned it the name of "Birmingham Bedford" in the trade. Since then the Austin has had successes of its own until the firm's resources have been diverted elsewhere as a result of the formation first of the British Motor Corporation and then the British Leyland group.

Opposite: The Austin Seven made a panel van of minute dimensions.

Below: The 14hp 15cwt light delivery van as turned out by Austin in 1908

By 1913 there was a substantial export market for the 15hp unit and this one was en route, before the days of ckd (completely knocked down) dispatch, to the Brazilian postal department.

Bottom left: The 1922 model of the agricultural tractor had patent steel wheels.

Below: The 1934 Austin 12/16 car chassis was the basis of this delivery van.

Bottom: Heavy commercial production resumed in 1939 — the end of the assembly line with the new 50cwt coming off in quantity.

BAT

One of the features of the road transport legislation of the thirties was the stress put on lightweight construction by the classification of vehicles with an unladen weight of 50cwt (later 3ton) as motor cars; they were thus eligible for operation at 30mph. For this opening market Harris & Hasell Ltd of Bristol, which had earlier held the agency for the American Reo Chassis, set itself out to cope by building the BAT (British Associated Transport) chassis. The target for production in the first year (1930) was 500 vehicles. Called the Cruiser or 1930-Model 3 chassis the specification had attractions. The RAC rating of the petrol engine was 27.3hp and the maximum output 59hp. Unfortunately this was one more case where high hopes were dashed by the economic circumstances of the day, the looming 1933 Road & Rail Traffic Act and the taxation threats of the Salter Report.

Below: The BAT Cruiser, on test for Modern Transport in 1929, soars over the railway bridge in the steep start of Succombs Hill, Warlingham. T. H. Everitt

Bean

Founded in 1901 as A. Harper & Sons Ltd, the firm of Bean Cars Ltd became interested in commercial vehicles during the 1920's. The object was to devise a universally acceptable chassis and at the close of the decade prototypes of the Empire chassis for 50cwt loads at home and 2ton on rougher roads overseas were to be seen under test — indeed, the Australian representative was definitely under orders to test to destruction. The eight vehicles totalled 150,000 miles of test running to the middle of 1929; one carried 52cwt on three journeys a week from the Midlands to London and each trip covered 238 miles in 10 hours. The 50cwt Empire was followed soon after by a 30cwt which made use of the 46bhp engine out of the Hadfield car of the Bean range; this was dropped to make use of the components in the light freight vehicles. As seen on the MODERN TRANSPORT test route the 30cwt was handicapped by a very high low-gear ratio, although it surmounted the 1 in 6 of Bug Hill in spanking style. The 1931 season saw a 20-25cwt chassis — the New Era — which performed vigorously on the 1 in 4½ of Succombs Hill, but which the journal (the initiator of tests of commercial vehicles) thought was good enough to justify the addition of four-wheel brakes and a self-starter. Financial events in the depression prevented the maker following up this idea.

Above: After the 50cwt Empire model the Bean commercial range was expanded by a 30cwt with the Hadfield car engine in 1930. The gear ratios were not quite right, but it went unfalteringly through the Miry Miriam watersplash (now closed to motor vehicles) on its Modern Transport test run.
T. H. Everitt

Below: In 1931 the New Era Bean truck for 20-25cwt loads made its appearance and is here seen in rural surroundings on the Kent and Surrey border.

Beardmore

It is curious how few of the great firms of general engineers have been happy when attempts were made to get into the specialist know-how of construction and marketing called for by the building of cars and commercial vehicles.

The Beardmore group was no exception, although it has retained a long connection with the cab trade. For the 1931 Commercial Motor Show the company took up production here of a range under Chenard-Walcker patents; William Beardmore & Co Ltd made arrangements for these to be wholly built in Britain. The largest was the Anaconda 15ton multi-wheeled outfit with a Meadows 115hp engine, a 20in single-plate clutch and a five-speed gearbox. A Python model for 12 to 15ton loads had a 95hp engine and the Cobra

10ton tractor unit had a Meadows four-cylinder 50hp engine. A Larkhall swan-neck drawbar transferred 15 per cent of the trailer load at 20mph to the rear wheels of the tractor; load transference increased on steep gradients. A Beardmore diesel engine was on the market in the middle of the 'thirties and was an accepted alternative in Albion models. The Beardmore railway traction diesel was a success in the USA.

The impressive Beardmore Anaconda 15ton tractor coupled to a semi-trailer. The petrol engine, of 115hp, was built by Meadows; chassis design incorporated Chenard-Walcker patents. The drawbar was by Larkhall. This unit was put into service in 1931 by the Rockware Glass Syndicate and had an unladen weight of 2ton 15cwt 1qr, with a legal maximum speed of 16mph.

Bedford and Chevrolet

Maker of the Bedford truck is Vauxhall Motors Ltd, which became established in the mid-nineteenth century as Alexander Wilson's Vauxhall Iron Works and turned from marine engines increasingly to petrol-engined cars from 1902 onwards. Success caused a move of the factory to Luton and it was at the end of the twenties that the General Motors Corporation of America acquired the business. For some time General Motors had been endeavouring to launch its Chevrolet commercial vehicle section in Britain — with a spectacular demonstration of its six-cylinder model, assembled at Hendon, climbing a flight of steps among other ploys and performing well for a road test up the "colonial" section of Old Chalky, near Westerham — but now

it was decided to redesign for the British market and to make and sell through the Vauxhall organisation a light lorry that would be inexpensive. A production line was set up in the Vauxhall Works at Luton and under the fresh territorial name of Bedford success was immediate. The 2-tonner emerged in 1931; soon afterwards the 30cwt and 12cwt models were available; the 8cwt came out in 1933 and a 3-tonner in 1934. The load limit rose to 5 tons in 1939 and soon after the war was over the 500 000th Bedford was completed. From that quantity production in a new factory at Dunstable has vastly increased and from being specialists in light vehicles the Bedford range covers the gamut of commercial and passenger vehicle operating needs.

Opposite: The new Chevrolet Six grips the imagination and a flight of steps at a sales demonstration in 1929 (Topical; Radio Times Hulton Picture Library).

Below: One of the first 3-ton Bedford trucks with long-wheelbase, delivered in 1934, at a Sussex quarry.

The 'Giraffe' was built by Bedford to satisfy a Ministry of Supply theory about wading military supplies ashore in the invasions we were committed to in World War II.

In the end the wading concept was superseded by the waterproofing theory and this view in Wardown Park shows how well a Bedford, waterproofed by Army personnel after Vauxhall instruction, could perform when submerged.

Opposite top: An original Bedford as a breakdown truck in the service of a pioneer Bedford agent, Scottish Motor Traction Co Ltd, tows Mons Meg, the famous Flanders gun, back to Edinburgh Castle after it had been mounted on a new carriage conforming to the original design and presented to the Castle by Sir William J. Thomson, in 1934 both Lord Provost of Edinburgh and chairman of Scottish Motor Traction.

Opposite centre: By 1938 the Bedford 3-tonner had assumed a modern frontal appearance.

Opposite bottom: The wartime Army truck had a utilitarian bonnet and a lively buckjumping performance on test.

Commer

Dating back to the early development of the mechanised load carrier in the internal combustion era, Commer Cars was a contraction of the official title of Commercial Cars Ltd adopted in 1905. The epicyclic Lindley gearbox with preselector was a feature of all the early models, which ran from 1 to 6ton capacity. The 1914-18 war output from the company's works at Luton comprised over 3000 four-ton vehicles. The expedient of early days for getting Commer vehicles out on the road was a hiring system through Commercial Car Hirers Ltd, but unfortunately this did not avail the company in the hard times after the 1914-18 war, when thousands of Army lorries were let loose on the home market. The Humber car group took the company over in 1926 and re-named its own Centaur Co Ltd of 1911 as Commer Cars Ltd. The Rootes group acquired Humber-Hillman-Commer in 1928 and thereafter immense strides were made with the brilliant ranges of

Centaur models and — just before the war — the very popular Superpoise vehicles. At one stage rather unimaginative model designations were used; the G6 was a short-wheelbase forward projecting engine model which catered for a design taste around 1930; the B3 of 1933 was a 3-tonner which went round the MODERN TRANSPORT test route powered by a Dorman-Ricardo oil engine. Then came more attractive model names such as the forward-control Raider, which we first came across inappropriately attached to a vehicle engaged in bulk delivery of school milk. Today Commer works under the Chrysler umbrella.

Opposite: The lightweight Centaur of 1932 was held to have a brilliant performance when put over the Modern Transport Derbyshire route.

Below: This veteran from the Commercial Cars days gave 14 years' service to the Gas Light & Coke Company in London. The Lindley pre-selective gear is by the driver's right hand and is mounted on the steering column.

The Commer Pug, with a 33ft turning circle, appeared in 1933 in the Carter Paterson parcels delivery fleet; it was classified CP by the owners, leaving the impression that it was a home-made vehicle.

The G3 conformed to a popular demand of 1930 that engines mounted forward of the front axle were an advantageous layout.

In Bowater-Lloyd service the LN5 forward-control model is seen picking up paper for a Fleet Street daily in 1937.

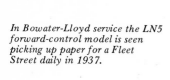

42

A Superpoise handling timber at Cardiff Docks in 1939

A wartime scene; a vehicle with masked headlights is propelled by the Government Mark VII gas producer. Fox Photos

Commer exports continued to selected countries during the war and this is a 1941 shot in the Port of London of a truck destined for South America.

Dennis

Trained as an ironmonger, John Dennis broke into cycle building in the cycling boom of 1895 and brought in his younger brother Raymond. From Speed King bicycles it was a small step to a motorised quadricycle and then a car. Dennis Bros Ltd produced its first commercial vehicle in 1904. The company did well with worm-drive buses, but load carriers were developed rapidly with a two-cylinder 14hp, and four-cylinder 20, 24 and 28hp models by 1906. The first Dennis fire engine incorporated an overdrive gearbox as early as 1908 as well as a Gwynne turbine pump which could push 400gal per min to a great height — over the dome of St Pauls was achieved in 1910. The War Department

3½ton subsidy type lorry of 1913 was turned out in enormous numbers — 7000 — for those pre-batch production days during the years of the first world war. During the depression of the postwar period 2½-tonners and municipal vehicles (cesspool emptiers, gully emptiers, refuse collectors) were designed and built. Load carrying came down to the low level of 30cwt later in the twenties but the mass-production methods of Morris and others were a warning light and by 1931 a 12ton six-wheeler was being marketed. But the bulk of Dennis output in the thirties was of modestly rated units — a four-wheeled freight vehicle using Lancet bus units and an elegant range of 2½ton models.

Opposite: The Dennis Light 4ton chassis at the 1935 Commercial Motor Show.

Below: The high-bonneted Dennis subsidy lorry of 1913 had a nominal load of 3½ton; some 7,000 were built during the 1914-18 war for the War Department.

Above: Fire engines have been a specialised product for over 60 years, but this was supplied to the London Fire Brigade in 1931.

Top left: Dennis reliability won Post Office favour; this mail van, seen flashing past on a 1972 Historic Commercial Vehicle Club occasion, was built in 1910. S. W. Stevens-Stratten.

Bottom left: The unloading of the spare wheel from behind the cab of the 12-tonner of 1933.

Below: Other municipal vehicles included gully emptiers which had tipping gear to dump the sludge.

Above: Ajax of 1938 represented the acme of Dennis design before the 1939-45 war turned Dennis production towards tanks.

Top left: Based on the Lancet bus chassis, this Dennis tilt van was engaged in long-distance haulage in 1934.

Bottom left: The 40-45cwt lorry on test for Modern Transport in the rugged North Downs country between Titsey Hill and Croydon Airport.

Left: The Pax 5-tonner was put on the market immediately after the war and a pre-production specimen is seen loaded with weights on test in the Hogs Back country in July, 1945.

49

Dodge

Famous American car firm of Dodge Brothers gained a foothold in Britain in 1922; its English company had some interlocking directorate with the corresponding English organisation of the Chrysler Corporation even before that swallowed Dodge in 1930. Dodge progress went through the stages of marketing a US-built truck chassis, building bodywork to match in London and then, after 1930, moving to the Kew works of Chrysler and getting cracking on a limited range of commercial vehicles, one of which is seen making the then perilous ascent of the 1 in 4½ of Succombs Hill, Warlingham. The smallest of these as seen in the early 'thirties were based on private car practice and for a time the driver-behind-engine concept prevailed up to the top of the range. With an element of British material in the construction, but US engines and gearboxes, the Surrey was brought in as a brand name in 1933. Developments of load capacity were offered in a semi-forward-control 5-tonner and this short-bonneted model became the first all-British Dodge in 1938 when it was fitted with a Perkins diesel engine. The Kew works were devoted very largely to aircraft construction in the 1939-45 war; as part of the London Aircraft Group units of Halifax bombers were produced. The subsequent career of Dodge and Fargo vehicles and their association with the Rootes group are matters outside this story.

A short-wheelbase semi-forward-control chassis as a 4 ton hydraulic tipper.

A 3 ton Dodge climbing Succombs Hill, Warlingham, in 1930. T. H. Everitt

Top left: Four years later another driver-behind-engine model surmounts the 1 in 4½ of Crown Ash Hill on the Modern Transport Surrey and Kent border test route. (Crown Ash Hill is now closed to motor vehicles)

Bottom left: This Dodge truck somehow made itself indispensable background to the hounds in John Peel's country.

Top: Tow-rope and a Dodge 4-5 tonner aid demolition work in 1937. Fox Photos

Above: Two panel vans on car chassis make high-speed transport for shaving tackle. Fox Photos

ERF

Enormous enthusiasm and a family row started this firm off in the tail of the industrial depression of the 'thirties. Mr Edwin R. Foden came from a family which had played an enormous part in the development of the steam road vehicle and which still saw something in it in the dawning diesel era. He decided to set up on his own and with no more than 20 on his total staff had turned out 14 vehicles by the end of the first year, 1933. Well-tried components were used and the motive units were from the already proven Gardner range of automotive diesel engines. Since then Rolls-Royce and Cummins engines have been used but we believe that all the models down to 1939 had Gardner units. It is certainly true to say that their merit for handling the maximum possible loads at that time permitted was recognised at a very early stage. The natural corollary was the four-wheeled ballasted tractor for trailer haulage and as it became widely accepted, the motive units of articulated outfits. Among original features was the half-cab model brought out at the end of 1938, unusual in freight vehicle construction, but suitable for pipe or girder carrying.

The early ERF load carriers were plain but sound and used Gardner engines, the reputation of which for reliability added to their credit.

Right: A half cab model produced in 1939.

Below: An ERF tractor about to make light of two heavily-loaded Dyson trailers.

Bottom: An ERF tractive unit with a low-loading semi-trailer for machinery carrying was added to the fleet of George H. C. Hind of Duddington, near Stamford, during the 1939-45 war. Gordon Turrill of Stamford

Foden

Steam tractors of high efficiency, due to a competent design of compound engine, were produced by Edwin Foden experimentally from 1882 onwards and as a regular production job from about five years later. In 1888 the firm was already confidently able to advertise that it had tried flexible spokes and abandoned the idea owing to "fatal defects." After the passage of the 1896 Locomotives on Highways Act thought went into designing a load-carrying vehicle and in 1901 a Foden lorry won a £250 award in War Office trials for a trouble-free run of 257 miles covered at about 6mph. Foden took over the Elworth works, Sandbach, of Plant & Hancock where he had been apprenticed and Fodens Ltd began lorry production in earnest in 1902. For many years the standard machines with cylinders and engine mounted on the boiler and flywheel just above the steering wheel, appealed to a wide market of heavy vehicle users. A complete redesign in the late twenties gave greater load space, with vertical boiler, underfloor engine and pneumatic tyres. But taxation tolled the knell of the steamer and the company introduced diesel vehicles, using the Gardner 6L2 72bhp engine, in 1931. At that year's Commercial Show the Speed-Six and Speed–Twelve steamers on pneumatic tyres made defiant gestures to the world. Later in Foden diesels the Dorman engine was also employed and for a very short period petrol-engined Fodens were offered. Subsequent engine developments included use of Rolls-Royce and in due time Cummins units, as well as — also after the time of these photographs — the brilliant Foden two-stroke diesel with exceptionally low specific weight per brake horsepower. In 1937 aluminium alloy designs were being used to lighten frames.

Not many people remember that a Foden petrol-engined job was marketed in the 1930's when many operators still wanted persuasion of the merits of the diesel.

The Foden story is sharply divided into the steam and diesel eras. The well-known steel-tyred overtype steam wagon design with a youthful hand ready for the wheel.

By 1927 cart steering had been superseded by the Ackermann type, solid rubber tyres were de rigeur, and a six-wheeler was on the market.

Above: A lorry and trailer outfit, new in 1932, for the milling division of the Co-operative Wholesale Society.

Top right: This six-wheeled diesel model of 1937 had an aluminium alloy frame which reduced chassis weight by 2½cwt.

Top centre: The dying gasp of Foden steam was a smart pneumatic-tyred undertype which was knocked out of British markets by taxation.

Top left: A strong frame with heavy bracing by stout cross-members at either end of the spring brackets was a feature of the Foden diesel

Left: The company turned over to a rugged quality-built Gardner-engined diesel in 1931. The long-life characteristics are emphasised by the company buying this pioneer back after 16 years' service in which it had run over 600 000 miles.

Far left: A Foden timber-hauling tractor with some steam design features still in evidence, as seen en route to a Historic Commercial Vehicle Club gathering in 1971. S. W. Stevens-Stratten.

FWD

For American Army transport in the 1914-18 war the Four Wheel Drive Auto Company of the United States turned out thousands of its vehicles with a track gauge of 4ft 8½in, so that they were easily adaptable as light locomotives if fitted with railway wheels. When they came out of the Army via the Slough reconditioning works a good many FWD entered years of service in road haulage, whether on local coal deliveries or with trailers on a long-distance milk run (these were still the days of churns) where they were not as useful as some owners hoped. Their high cabs were apt to do strange things to overhanging half-timbered cottages in winding country lanes. The English company, Four Wheel Drive Motors Ltd, began work from Slough in 1921 and some very ingenious adaptations, with four-wheeled rear bogies, rear crawler tracks and chain-wound balloon tyres, were demonstrated by the enterprising Charles Cleaver. Rail adaptations were marketed by Hardy Railmotors and eventually some of these ideas were embodied in AEC railcar designs. After numerous esoteric applications the FWD as such faded from the scene and no lorries can be traced after those backed by AEC in the 1932-36 period.

The typical FWD 4ton lorry in civilian service, with cab over engine, gearbox amidships and drive shafts running diagonally to each wheel.

A pneumatic-tyred version of the FWD truck hauling a Hardy rail-mounted locomotive unit.

Left: A basically six-wheeled unit converted to tracked drive showing its capacity for hauling three trailers.

Bottom left: There was a market in the adaptations built at Slough for side-tippers. There were no such complications as electrical equipment and oil lamps were the order of the cabless day when drivers provided their own oilskins for defence against the wet.

Below: This contrivance could deposit a load of bricks neatly on a pallet, right way up. The archaic artillery wheels have given place to solid-tyred steel-spoked wheels. Cecil H. Greville.

Ford

Having far-sightedly got into mass production at a very early stage Henry Ford exported cars to England in 1904 and began to assemble at Trafford Park in 1911. Four years later a Model T 7cwt van was produced and soon afterwards a stretched version rated at 1ton was available. Until the Model A (10cwt to 30cwt) of 1928 two-speed epicyclic gearboxes, pedal controlled, featured in these Ford commercials. The Ford Motor Co Ltd took over from Ford Motor Co (England) Ltd in 1928 and the Dagenham works went into production in 1931. By 1932 the company was producing the Model B 3-tonner and almost immediately the 5-ton six-wheelers appeared. The Sussex had double-drive and the Surrey single. The latter county title was also chosen by Dodge, but Ford was not at that time a member of the Society of Motor Manufacturers & Traders, the coordinating body in these matters. In 1935 a two-axle chassis in models suitable for 2 to 5ton loads appeared and as with the six-wheelers a 24hp four-cylinder or 30hp V8 petrol engine were offered as alternative power units. In the same year a three-wheeled Ford Tug appeared using parts common to the 1933 5cwt van which itself was based on the 8hp car. Diesel engines (first Perkins and then Ford's own) did not figure in the Ford range until after the war, when the adoption of Thames as a brand name linked a series of models with the extremely self-sufficient works on the riverside at Dagenham.

A 2ton van in the service of an egg merchant.

Top: An Albion 4ton overtype (engine alongside driver) of 1929. They were among the first forward control vehicles to become popular and were originally manufactured with solid tyres. With a 4/5ton payload, a wheelbase of 11ft 9in and a load space of 14ft 9in, the vehicles had a turning circle of approx 12ft.

Above: A 3½ton 1932 Dennis van fitted with a 4cyl petrol engine. The chassis had servo assisted hydraulic brakes and cost £555, plus an additional £25 for the all steel cab. This one was operated by a well known departmental store.

Top: A Sentinel DG4 steam wagon of 1930, a type once popular with contractors brewers and many other operators. These vehicles had a surprising turn of speed and were quieter than many of the commercial vehicles on the roads today.

Above: The Scammell Rigid-4 was designed in 1929 for the transport of 6ton loads at high speeds — it was capable of 40mph on the level and could maintain an average of 27mph or 23mph when pulling a 6ton loaded trailer. It was powered by a 4cyl 80bhp petrol engine having a consumption of 8mpg. The wheelbase was 17ft.

A Model T restored with loving care; this was available as a commercial for light loads from 1913. S. W. Stevens-Stratten.

The 1928 Model A 2-tonner with Barco extension to carry a two-horse box. S. W. Stevens-Stratten.

The 30cwt truck was given a rousing introduction in 1931 by climbs of famous West Country test hills. One carried a Fordson tractor and the other a 32cwt load of ballast plus nine well-grown men; they toiled up Porlock, Lynton and, as seen here, Beggars Roost, with stops and restarts to show there was no deception.

Below: The Ford Tug three-wheeler with two-wheeled trailer was designed for a 2 ton payload and could be turned in a 21 ft circle. This 1935 rival to other substitutes for the horse and cart had a quick coupling device for dropping and picking-up the trailer.

Bottom: A low-loading Dyson machinery trailer, 2 ft 7½ in to the platform, with four wheels in parallel at the rear end, shod with twin tyres, was attached to a Fordson power unit and was good for loads up to 8 ton.

Above: The lorry assembly line at Ford Works, Dagenham, in 1935.

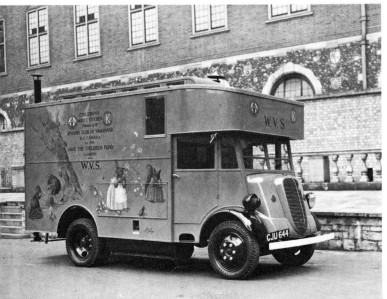

Far left: Loading a Fordson six-wheeler in a sand quarry in 1936

Right: A Thames mobile kitchen presented during the war to the Save the Children Fund in London by the Kiwanis Club of Vancouver, British Columbia.

69

Fowler

The Fowler organisation that took a part in the prewar lorry market was of respectable antiquity, the limited company of John Fowler & Co (Leeds) Ltd having been registered in 1886. Steam tractors and ploughing machinery gave way, in time for the 1931 Commercial Motor Show, to a heavy range of oil-engined chassis. The 6-7 ton, capable of hauling a trailer, was a semi-forward control vehicle of massive frontal appearance. The company's choice of oil engine was a six-cylinder unit, the cylinders being $4\frac{3}{8}$ in diameter by 7 in stroke and having patent cavity pistons. The same engine went into a 10-12 ton rigid six-wheeler. The

engine was designed suitably for fully forward-control layouts as there were no auxiliaries on the offside. After 1934 both steam and oil-engined goods vehicles disappeared from the scene in favour of agricultural tractors.

A massively handsome Fowler diesel-engined lorry and trailer put on the road in 1932 by a haulier with a daily service from London to Norwich.

A stop-and-restart demonstration on a 1 in 3 gradient, where diesel engine and gear ratio combined to give an effective performance.

Plunging into rough country on a convincing test of the Fowler six-wheeler's capabilities on site work.

Garner

A firm which had a number of vicissitudes but
which over various periods produced
interesting vehicles began as Moseley Motor
Works in 1907 and changed its title to Henry
Garner Ltd two years later. Maximum output
was in the lush twenties as Garner Motors Ltd,
the name assumed in 1927. Then in 1933 the
business was absorbed by Sentinel and
eventually — after the war — Garner traditions
could be traced in underfloor-engined goods
vehicles built at Shrewsbury. In the meantime
a quite "with it" (for the 'thirties) range of
lorries appeared under the Garner name,
ceasing, however, with the outbreak of the
1939-45 war.

On the 13ft 8in wheelbase 6AX chassis this cattle
wagon was mounted with a body 16ft 10in wide and
6ft 6in high.

The JO6 model Garner made a point in 1932 of
engine accessibility.

An AE type with 11ft wheelbase had what must seem a peculiar body for a sand and ballast contractor.

Bottom left: A big Garner six-wheeled chassis going through its repertoir of roadholding versatility on Old Chalky. Topical

Below: The 1937 Garner range had a currently "with it" radiator design.

Garrett

The Garrett business at Leiston in Suffolk was founded in 1778 and so could claim to be a father of agricultural engineering establishments. Richard Garrett & Sons Ltd was registered in 1897. After the 1896 Act it was natural to find the firm in the steam wagon field as well as involved in traction engine production. A stayless firebox and a three-cylinder compound engine (soon converted to a two-cylinder job) were among interesting features. The Suffolk Punch tractor, with chimney at the back and motor car steering and controls at the front was another original piece of design in the 1920s. In 1922 battery-electric tenders were built and proved long-lasting. Whereas the Garrett range of steamers with pressed steel disc wheels looked heavily formidable, the company was simultaneously building an elegant range of passenger vehicles in the shape of electric

trolleybuses. In 1929 one of the steam lorries was transformed into an oil-engined unit and this was among the earliest diesel-engined freight road vehicles to go to work on public roads in Britain; it was in the own-account fleet of Barford & Perkins of Peterborough, a member of the Agricultural & General Engineers group. By 1931 a 6 ton Garrett lorry powered by a Blackstone BHV6 six-cylinder diesel engine had been shown at Olympia, alongside an industrial tractor driven by an Aveling Invictar four cylinder diesel engine. But the first love, the steamer, brought up to date as a six-wheeled pneumatic-tyred vehicle, was still prominent. As a member of the Beyer Peacock group, however, road vehicles took up an ever smaller part of the activities and disappeared from the market before the 1939 war.

A steam-powered Garrett six-wheeler as beautifully restored by enthusiasts for rally purposes. R. G. Pratt.

Below: Garrett produced a pioneer oil-engined vehicle during 1929; it was the steamer with the boiler replaced by the diesel engine.

Bottom left and right: The new range of diesel lorries was accompanied by an industrial tractor and a roadless tractor, also oil-engined.

Gilford

The Gilford Motor Co Ltd, which started off as E. B. Horne & Company in 1926, rose with the ascendance of the pneumatic-tyred long-distance coach. Six-cylinder petrol engines and refined details, mainly of US designed or produced components and including Gruss auxiliary air springs over the front leaf springs, at a very reasonable capital cost made it attractive and some very large fleets were put to work. Gilford ventures into front-wheel-drive double-deck buses and the use of Tangye oil engines were not so successful and not many people in the industry today remember the essays into freight vehicles. A horsebox was shown at Olympia in 1931, where a two-stroke six-cylinder diesel appeared on the Gilford stand. The 3ton model was offered at the 1933 Commercial Motor Show; the OS4 had a four-cylinder petrol engine rated at

24.2hp. Wheelbases from 8ft 5in to 13ft were offered. Earlier the 168SD 32 seat bus chassis had been offered as a load carrier and a little fleet of tank wagons was built up. But the front-wheel drive and the diesel models failed to get off the ground in the way they deserved; manufacture at High Wycombe came to an untimely end in 1937.

A Gilford 168SD 32-seat coach chassis adapted as a tanker for petrol distribution.

The Gilford AS6 under test; the driver is Captain Richard Twelvetrees who inaugurated commercial vehicle testing. T. H. Everitt.

Guy

Sydney Slater Guy, who had been a chief designer with Sunbeam, resigned his job as works manager there in 1914 to embark on manufacture on his own. He had ideas on overhead camshafts, three-point suspension of engine and gearbox on a subframe and overdrive top gears. Not many of his first 30cwt commercials got on the road before the factory was commandeered for armament production. So Guy began all over again in 1919 and this time built a 2½-tonner. A man with a strong feeling for the countryside, he produced an estate lorry for farm work with spud tracks, a unit with Roadless half tracks and an articulated outfit. Still in the agricultural development class came a Guy version of the Stronach-Dutton road-rail tractor carried on narrow-gauge railway bogies. In 1922 the best medium for house-to-house calls was a battery-electric and so Guy produced a battery-powered 3-ton refuse collector. Some of the early vehicles

were exported and a 3-tonner that went to a South African haulier in 1921 was still going 36 years later! The six-wheeler came out of the Guy works in 1925, showing further the firm's capacity for originality, and the Goliath was a notable freight model of 1931. The Red Indian became the Guy symbol, with "feathers in our cap" to mark the achievements. In the thirties there was the extremely flexible eight-wheeled cross-country vehicle and, in contrast, the lightweight four-wheeled Otter (6ton load, weight under 2½ton unladen, thus qualifying for the 30mph class and £28 tax). Then the Vixen and later the military Vix-Ant provided some popular models. Guy output was renewed during the war (1941 onwards) for civilian freight and passenger requirements and before the company went into the Jaguar group reached, with diesel-engined versions, up to the 24ton gross class and to 105-passenger double-deck buses for South Africa.

A Guy Vixen supplied in 1939 to a Wolverhampton timber merchant.

Top: In 1936, Morris Commercial introduced their long
wheelbase 4ton chassis, which would allow a pantechnicon
body having 1,100 cu. ft. of space. The overall length
was 21ft and as the unladen weight was less than 50cwt,
such vehicles could legally travel at 30mph.

Above: A 20/25cwt delivery van of 1935. This Commer
has a body designed to the operators specification, and was
typical of the period.

Top: A Thornycroft Taunus, a type introduced in 1933, which had the front axle set back so that with a 13ft 6in wheelbase, a 16ft 6in platform could be fitted and the carrying capacity kept at 6/7ton. Alternative 4cyl or 6cyl petrol engines could be fitted or a diesel engine. The example depicted here is fitted with a four compartment, 1,500 gallon tank for the Anglo-American Oil Co. Ltd.

Above: A Commer series N, 1½/2ton vehicle which was introduced at the Commercial Motor Show in 1935. This is one of 30 such vehicles operated by a soft drink manufacturer.

Top: A Model B Guy 2 to 3 ton lorry supplied in 1921 to Knight Cartage Ltd, of Uitenhage, South Africa, in place of horse transport on a contract for South African Railways and hauling an ex-horse cart as a drawbar trailer, was still at work 36 years later.

Above: Guys of the 1924-29 period in the fleet of Chambers & Marsh just before the war; their daily work was the delivery of overhanging loads of timber, joinery and glazing to rough sites on new estates.

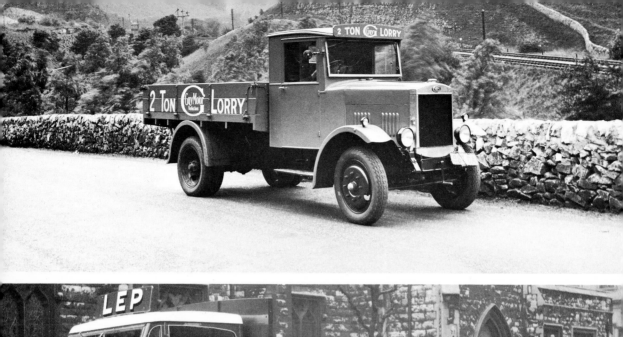

Top left: A 2ton Guy on test in Derbyshire in 1932

Centre left: A prewar Guy Fox six-wheeler in the service of a well-known firm of shipping agents.

Bottom left: A Wolf tractor and furniture trailer outfit supplied in 1941 for removal work.

Right: A prewar Guy Wolf seen on an HCVC run to Brighton at Pease Pottage in 1972. S. W. Stevens-Stratten.

Below: The Guy Vix-Ant wartime model on the 1 in 3 hairpin of Bwlch-y-Groes near Llangollen getting on and on and up and up with a 4ton load in 1941.

Halley

It is curious that apart from Albion no native-based motor industry has survived long in Scotland. Of the others Halley was the longest survivor and after a start on steam succeeded in carrying its radiator badge into the era of completely modern looking pneumatic-tyred vehicles. Moreover, the factory was absorbed by its Scottish competitor; the works at Yoker, being close to those of Albion at Scotstoun, were physically immediately useful to the new owners as integrated c. k. d. packing plant and for other handy extensions. The first Halley concern, Halley's Industrial Motors, Ltd, started up in 1906 and the re-registration as Halley Motors Ltd took place after 21 years. Some of the earlier Halley lorries had pleasing front ends and radiators and bonnets reminiscent of the 1912 Daimler bus, but with a bold script 'Halley' cast on the top header. Later this was changed for a sharp-ended radiator block with a silhouette like a Lea Francis car. Output of Halley vehicles eventually ceased in 1935.

Hallford

Although the firm of J & E Hall, Ltd, of Dartford was formed in 1900 it had already established a reputation in the shipping industry for high-quality design, largely with refrigerating machinery. In the early part of the second quinquennium of this century interest turned to road vehicles and they took part in early petrol-electric transmission experiments for Thomas Tilling Ltd, a horse bus proprietor who wanted to make the transition to motor driving easy for its men by removing the intricacies of clutch and gearbox from the vehicle. The result was highly satisfactory and was called "Queenie" by the men because of its quiet and docile habits. Large-scale production was eventually in the hands of Tilling-Stevens Motors at Maidstone but J & E Hall continued its interest in Hallford chassis production, some going to bus undertakings, but a number being used for freight carrying. By far the largest batch of these went to the War Department during the 1914-18 war and one of these rugged three-tonners is depicted in restored livery as seen at a rally. Many regret that the difficult post-war period brought an end to vehicle manufacture at Dartford; the maker is still engaged in movement through its escalator manufacturing division.

Left: In 1931 this six-wheeled bus chassis was provided with a body which carried six tons of stock as a travelling confectionery shop.

Bottom left: A 1929 YL type van revived to take part in a rally forty years later. It was found in an orchard before rebuilding sunk to the axles in the ground. S. W. Stevens-Stratten.

Below: One of the Halley types that emerged between the wars — a solid-tyre veteran employed by the Dundee depot of Whitbread.

Below right: The Hallford 3-tonner for Army use in the 1914-18 war as restored and seen in a manoeuvrability test at Spurrier Works, Leyland, in 1958 on the very first Historic Commercial Vehicle Club rally.

Hornsby

For many years I have cherished a photograph
of a genus of mechanical dinosaur, with
boiler-mounted steam engine and what is
commonly referred to as caterpillar track,
cavorting across a piece of rough country. I
had forgotten its origin beyond its association
with the Yukon and was inclined to attribute it
to industrial development during the Klondyke
gold rush in the latter part of the nineties.
Further inquiry shows it to have been built as
late as 1909 by the Grantham firm of Richard
Hornsby & Sons Ltd to haul coal wagons over
difficult terrain to and from a North-West
Canada mining project. The Roberts
track-laying equipment had actually been
developed on Hornsby's heavy oil-engined
tractors, but no British manufacturer (nor the
Army authorities) was sufficiently seized of
its merits and rights in it were eventually
transferred to the US-based Holt Caterpillar
Company, which took its title from the
British Army's spontaneous nickname for the
track. It is the basis of the British Army tank
of 1916, also developed by Hornsby at
Lincoln, and many modern track-laying
vehicles. The first patents on steam traction
engines incorporating Hornsby's name were
taken out in 1863 and he and his partners
were in production the following year. Today
at Lincoln Ruston & Hornsby — as the firm
has been since 1918 — is still interested in
traction — big diesel engines for railway
service and air-cooled automotive adaptations
tried out in buses and lorries.

*Not a Frankenstein monster, but a Hornsby
steam-powered tractor intended for coal haulage over
rough tracks in North-West Canada. The track
equipment was developed in the British Army tank of
1916, seven years later, and was the basis of the
American range of Caterpillar vehicles.*

International Harvester

Having made its fame out of reapers in the great wide open spaces of the prairies it was natural for the International Harvester Company to go on to tractors for agricultural use and then to break into industry with an industrial tractor. The conversion to pneumatic tyres on the tractor was made by 1927, and by that time the International load-carrying chassis were on the British market; the SF 2½ton Speed Truck chassis is a model we remember — a typical light vehicle of North American design. During the following year the company got on the map with the exploits of a 1-tonner which crossed the Sahara from North Africa and reached Tanganyika. A service station was opened in London and there was an impressive model, the Six Speed Special. In the early thirties the load ratings increased — the AW2 was a 30-40 cwt three-way tipper and there was a 5-tonner

with a six-cylinder 65bhp engine. In 1931 the LMSR had a specially-adapted International tractor shunting wagons at Crown Street, Liverpool, and ten years later an International Harvester lorry chassis equipped with a Bay City crane was helping the LMS to cope with the surge of wartime traffic. Although International Harvester was basically a Chicago and an Akron, Ohio, company, its factories spread from the US into Canada, with plant at Hamilton, Ontario. Manufacture in Britain has been carried out at Doncaster in the postwar years.

A Gravesend timber merchant operated this 1929 model International Speed Truck in a fleet of Internationals.

In solid tyre days a cab-fitted 10-20 International hauls a two-wheeled trailer for Settle Rural District Council.

Right: One of the early distributors of bottled milk in Staffordshire used a solid-tyred version of the International lorry which was on the British market from about 1927 onwards.

Below: Pneumatic-tyred International tractor positioning a wagon in Liverpool Docks for a Vulcan locomotive for India to be loaded on board ship.

Below right: Some of the new range of International Harvesters working for the London Midland & Scottish Railway were fitted with flanged wheels outside the road wheels and one is seen here hauling wagons at Crown Street, Liverpool, in 1931.

Top left: A handsome International seen in London in 1935.

Left: A semi-forward-control modification which went to a corn merchant not far from Burnley, where the vehicle was registered.

Top: Wartime traffic on the LMS was speeded by a Bay City crane mounted on an International Harvester chassis.

Above: The K8 International at work in 1942 for a Leytonstone firm of builders' merchants; addresses are blanked out following the panic about German paratroops in 1940.

Karrier

My first acquaintance with Karrier lorries was through an article describing railway cartage vehicles which showed a massive Karrier 5-tonner belonging to the Great Central Railway with the driver sitting on top of the engine, like the Wolseley bus of a few years previously, and some orthodox lighter delivery vans in London & South Western Railway livery. Both were chain-driven in the convention of heavy units in 1914. The manufacturer of these vehicles had a diversified business making railway fog-signalling machines and detonators, registered in 1904 as Clayton & Co (Huddersfield) Ltd and not taking on the name Karrier Motors Ltd until its postwar restart in 1920.

Mr. R. F. Clayton left when Karrier Motors Successors, controlled by Humber Ltd, Rootes group member, was formed in 1934, and he revivified Tilling-Stevens at that time. The title Karrier Motors was again adopted in 1935 and manufacture was carried out at Luton in association with the Rootes Commer business. Karrier was an early exponent of the rigid six-wheeled chassis, one passenger model earning the spontaneous title of "the submarine" at a Commercial Motor Show. In 1932 the K type chassis was done over and

entirely modernised as the 6-ton four-wheeled Consul. It still had to be hand-started but it was a cab-over-engine vehicle of modern appearance. The end-of-year corollary was the six-wheeled Consort freighter with a gross load of 11 tons, but this was powered by a Gardner 6LW oil engine and was equipped with an overspeed top gear and attained 47mph on test. There was an electric starter, it goes without saying, but the clutch was a fabric-lined inverted cone. Railway interest in a motor vehicle which would replace the horse in the horse-hauled railway collection and delivery service produced the three-wheeled Karrier Cob in 1930; coupling gear enabled it to pick up trailers or adapted horse vans. In 1936 a four-wheeled Bantam tractor was brought out which gradually superseded Cob production. As we drew nearer to the war the municipal vehicles Karrier produced in conjunction with the Yorkshire Patent Steam Wagon Co Ltd took on a more sinister line and took part in demonstrations of washing poison gas from streets among other civil defence (or as they then were, arp) exercises. During the war attention turned to military requirements, and the four-wheel drive K6 was among the products.

Opposite page: Besides three-wheeled tractors the Karrier business, as a part of the Rootes group included the Bantam four-wheeler in its range. Wordie & Co Ltd operated from Glasgow and dated back to 1700, but became railway-owned in 1932.

Right: A three-wheeled 2-tonner for refuse collection was based on the Colt chassis at the same period.

Below: The Karrier CYR type refuse collector of 1930.

Left: The year 1932 saw the Karrier Consul four-wheeled six-tonner and the six-wheeled version christened Consort; the latter is seen on a Modern Transport test between Buxton and Bakewell on the "road of the Seven Hills".

Far left: Pavement washing after a simulated poison-gas attack — a timely demonstration by a Karrier-Yorkshire unit under the stress of war threats in 1938.

Centre left: A Karrier Cob three-wheeled tractor on a quickly-detachable semi-trailer handling tram rails in Leeds.

Bottom left: The mechanical power could be detached under the Karrier economical refuse collection system of 1937 and replaced by a horse for house-to-house visits, leaving the powered motive unit to make the run to the dust destructor at higher speed.

A 1943 four-wheel-drive Karrier, the K6, gets into the rough and out again successfully.

Kerr Stuart

While the Associated Equipment Co Ltd and others were investigating ways of using otherwise unwanted cuts of hydrocarbon oil or petrol distillation, commonly known as derv or diesel fuel, by developing the high-speed compression-ignition engine, an enterprising locomotive builder in Staffordshire had also been making plans. The firm was Kerr Stuart, which from the eighties had been in business selling railway equipment in Glasgow, and moved to a pottery engineers' works at Stoke-on-Trent in 1892. Somewhat intermittently in the next three decades it obtained valuable orders which included the world's last and largest single locomotives, four 100ton 4-2-2s built for China in 1910. I treasure a catalogue of its standard steam contractors' engines; it was in this department that K. W. Willans, designer of early Sentinel industrial locomotives, produced ideas for high-pressure geared steam locomotives, diesel locomotives and one of the earliest diesel lorries to get on the road. Thought up in 1928,

it was seen when a prototype as a 6-tonner. Trials began with a six-cylinder Helios diesel engine but a quick change was made to the four-cylinder 60hp McLaren-Benz diesel which was governed down to 800rpm. A little air-cooled JAP engine was used to start the diesel up, as electric starting peppy enough to overcome the diesel's compression did not appear to be available to Willans. Chain drive to the back axle gave an old-fashioned touch to the vehicle, but it had four-wheel brakes. The brake pedal had to be stood upon in the prototype but servo-assistance improved the production batch, some of which went to such famous firms as Whitbreads. Fuel cost only 4d a gallon in 1929 and it ran 10 to 12 miles to the gallon, even if it sometimes blew its cylinder heads skyhigh. Just as the company was going to develop its new lines, backed with cash receipts from a big GWR order for pannier tanks its activities were brought to a sudden halt through the intervention of a bank.

Back in 1902 the Long Acre Motor Car Co Ltd was formed as a natural corollary of that Covent Garden thoroughfare having become known as a street of motor car dealers. The firm had a broader horizon than the mere selling of cars and on October 8th, 1903, simplified its name to Lacre Motor Car Co Ltd; unintentionally, no doubt, this gave the impression that some French expertise was incorporated and we have heard cognoscenti who pronounce "Lacre" as if it were a French name. Before the 1914 war a substantial commercial vehicle was in production from a factory at Letchworth; in the convention of many makers of the time, final drive was by chain. A range from 10cwt to 6ton was advertised and the 38hp 5-tonner was turned out for the War Department. The London office was in what is now York Way, Kings Cross, and it was from there that Lacre Lorries, Ltd, as it became in 1928, was operated, although a move to a new works at Welwyn was soon accomplished. The new company tended to concentrate on municipal vehicles for health and sanitary services — its pre-1914 predecessor had listed tower wagons, tank wagons, prison vans, vacuum sewage plants, fire engines and ambulances in sales propaganda — and especially on street sweepers, for which it attained an enviable reputation for excellence.

Léft: A Kerr-Stuart diesel lorry working for a roadstone merchant in 1930.

Below: A Lacre 2ton van of 1913, which saw service in France in the 1914-18 war, makes a comeback, after four years of restoration work, nearly 60 years later in an HCVC event. S. W. Stevens-Stratten.

Latil

When I was in road haulage I laughed my head off at a demonstration driver of a Latil four-wheel drive tractor who got up against a stable wall and couldn't get away. The vehicle had four-wheel steering, too, and as the front wheels turned away from the wall the rear wheels turned into it. With one set of steering locked it was a useful unit, but then had a somewhat larger turning circle. Latil Industrial Vehicles Ltd was in business in England from 1927, but the company had manufactured in France from 1904 onwards, lorries being marketed as Blum-Latil at first. From 1932 to 1939 the Latil was turned out by Shelvoke & Drewry Ltd at Letchworth and was given the subsidiary name of "Traulier". Some of these tractors were produced with both road and railway wheels, four-wheel bogies with flanges surrounding the pneumatic tyred wheel, somewhat akin to the Evans Auto-railer that ran in combined bus and railcar services in

North America, and were to be seen doing industrial shunting. The 1933 model was equipped with a four-cylinder side-valve monobloc Latil petrol engine which developed 50bhp at 2000rpm. Low or high gear ratios could be selected (by the use of some dexterity) and a trailer giving an all-up weight of 16½ton was taken over the 'Modern Transport' test route — at up to 20mph on the level and 2mph up 1 in 6. A 22ton all-up load was promised. But the poor braking capacity of the outfit with 75per cent of that weight was criticised — no doubt due to the brakes on the trailer provided. The steering of the Traulier was good, but internal gears in the wheels made the tractor turning circle a minimum of 27ft. A ton or so of ballast (or useful load if possible) could be carried over the rear wheels to assist adhesion. Low-loading lorries with large front wheels and small rear carrying wheels were also a Latil speciality.

A Latil Traulier tractor attached by drawbar to a Great Western Railway low-loading machinery carrier.

During the Shelvoke & Drewry association with Latil in 1936 this works shunter, made up of a Traulier mounted on flanged wheels, to constitute a Loco Traulier, was put to work.

LO CO
TRAULIER

DGJ402

Leyland

By merit of design, by well-conceived organisation and sheer hard salesmanship Leyland has been outstanding among British commercial vehicle manufacturers and became in 1968 a leading component in the vast British Leyland Motor Corporation. The signs of this were upon the Lancashire Steam Motor Company's products from its start in 1896 — and steam wagons continued to be built until the twenties, having been the subject of experiment by James Sumner, one of the founders, back in 1884. George and Henry ('Henry the Second') Spurrier joined him and brought in their father, Henry the First. Henry the Second's enormous work for the commercial motor vehicle development of this country is recognised by the Chartered Institute of Transport's Spurrier Memorial Lecture and its associated scholarships. First petrol vehicle out of Leyland (Leyland Motors Ltd was a name adopted in 1907) was a 30cwt job which earned itself the name 'Pig' on birth in 1904. But from 1905 onwards the successful 24bhp (Y series) 3-tonner, X-type (35bhp, 3½ton), and U-type (50bhp, 5ton) carried fame far and wide and an 85bhp, 60mph fire engine put out a fire in Dublin during its handing over ceremony in 1910. The success of a demonstration to the War Department secured orders for a 3-tonner

under the subsidy scheme and this 'RAF Leyland' was quantity-produced — 5,932 from August 1914 to November 1918, of which 5,411 went into Royal Air Force service. Variations came after the war, including the P type and its remarkable overtype modification where the driver was perched up in the air, to give more body space. By 1929 we were almost in modern times, with the freight range incorporating Bison, Buffalo, Bull and Hippo, the latter a six-wheeled 12-tonner. The Bellem oil engine was put through its paces by a research department in 1925, but Leyland was not really satisfied with oil engine performance until the early thirties and offered a high camshaft petrol engine, the Mark III, as late as 1937. Pretty big outputs not only of conventional lorries, going up to the eight-wheeled Octopus, and buses, but of various twin-steer jobs were achieved in the late thirties including a Twin-Steered Beaver and then an improved unit, the Steer. In the meantime a freight-carrying Cub, followed by the 6-ton Lynx for an unladen weight of 50cwt, had been a popular riposte to the lightweight mass-production market.

A coal gas or petrol experiment with a Beaver in 1934.

Based on the celebrated RAF subsidy model, this Carter Paterson vehicle was demonstrating the swop body principle in the 1930's.

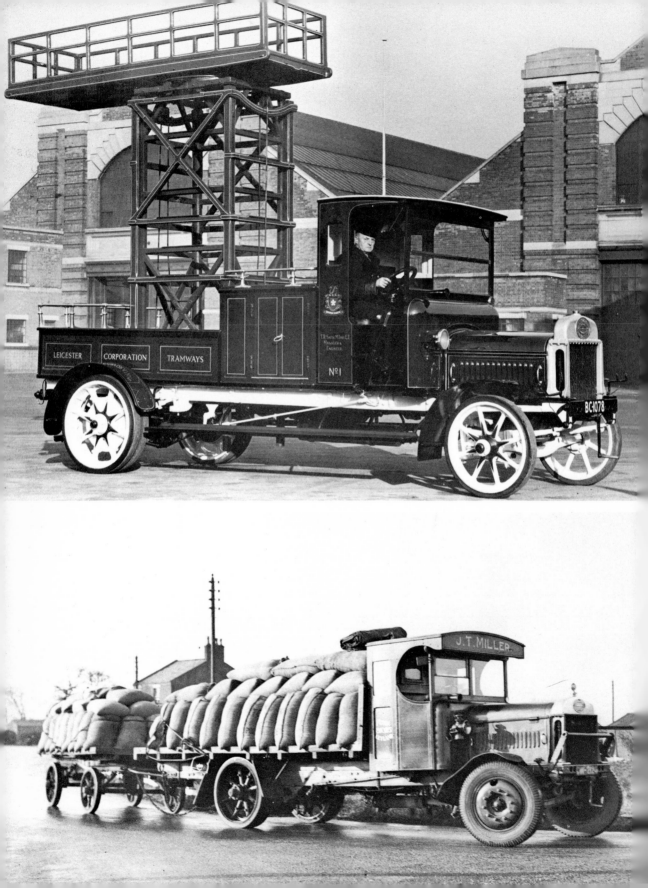

Above: Seen on the 'Modern Transport' Derbyshire circuit, this was modernised in 1932 with pneumatic tyres and Dorman-Ricardo diesel engine.

Right: The P class was an overtype of the 1920's in which the driver was perched high in the air.

Top left: A classic Neo-Georgian Leyland with huge radiator header, restored beautifully by Leicester Corporation transport staff before going to Leicester Museum. It was in tramways department service from 1911 to the end of the line in 1949 and was then used for a few more years as a depot lorry.

Left: A 1914 specimen that in 1934 was still running 500 miles a week and, with a trailer, shifting 10ton loads.

Left: A ten-wheeled tractor-trailer combination specially built for oil field work during 1934. It had an 11 litre petrol engine, 150bhp, for a 15ton load.

Far left: The engine-mounted-ahead-of-the-front-axle vogue was met by Leyland in 1931 with the Buffalo.

Below left: The Leyland Cub, originated at Kingston as a small normal control unit, quickly grew up to be a driver-beside-engine-type. This one with a horse-box body was photographed in 1933.

Below: A driver-behind-engine Cub, produced as a six-wheeler with 18ft body for 24ft long timber.

Bottom: A 1933 export: Leyland Badger and trailer in the service of Victorian Railways, Australia.

McCurd

W. A. McCurd was one of the automobile engineers of the Edwardian and early Georgian years whose ideas on commercial vehicles were both sound and progressive. He produced some neat and effective chassis designs, with a faint resemblance, owing to the radiator shape, to the 1912 Daimlers of the Searle regime. On April 10th, 1913, the McCurd business was turned into a limited company which purchased from its founder

"certain rights, benefits and information relating to the manufacture of self-propelled vehicles" — in modern terms, 'know-how' — and from headquarters in the Tottenham Court Road area of London brisk business was done for some years; lorries with McCurd on the radiator became a familiar sight and the chassis was also used for buses by such discerning operators as the Walfords of the Ortona Motor Company of Cambridge.

Below: A 1913 McCurd 5 ton van in the livery of le Tate & Lyle Ltd, taking part in a 1972 HCVC rally. This vehicle was derelict from 1927 to 1964. S. W. Stevens-Stratten

Right: The imposing diesel-engined McLaren haulage unit was based on steam traction engine tradition and with its 125hp power output could be relied on to haul heavy indivisible loads of over 100 ton.

McLaren

Unlike several firms that specialised in steam traction engines J. & H. McLaren Ltd, of Midland Engine Works, Leeds, had no petrol lorry ambitions. The company was in the steam traction engine and steam roller business from 1877 to 1930 and was also interested in an oil-engined agricultural tractor. Its speciality from the traction engine stage was to substitute oil engines in steam traction engines, providing special frames to hold them together and do what the boiler had served to do as a structural member. Culmination of this was a design of oil-engined tractor for heavy indivisible loads. It included a 125hp McLaren — Ricardo 5MR oil engine as motive unit, placed amidships, and designed to run at 1000rpm. It was massive — 17ft 11in in overall length, 8ft 5in wide and 9ft 9in over the cab roof — and the overall weight was 12ton 15cwt unladen, 13ton 8cwt in working order and 17ton with ballast in position. The rear wheels — twin solid-tyred — were 1ft 4in wide and 6ft in diameter. On test it hauled a 109ton load satisfactorily and was stated to be much cheaper on fuel than a steam unit, even though it used about 1¼gal a mile. The tractive effort in first gear (123.4 to 1 ratio) was 17,200lb at 1.76mph and in fourth (22.1 to 1) it could achieve 9.82mph, but exert a drawbar pull of only 3,090lb. With a winding rope and double purchase snatchblock it could exert a pull of 40,800 lb.

Maudslay

Rationalisation swallowed Maudslay in the Associated Commercial Vehicles group, in other words AEC, but its factory long contributed to British Leyland output. The brilliant Maudslay engineering family gave rise both to the commercial vehicle activities of Maudslay Motor Co Ltd (formed 1907) from 1904 and to the Standard popular car, which prepared the way for a Leyland light van after Standard-Triumph joined that group. Among the engineering forebears were Maudslay & Field, a partnership which rebuilt and improved a Gurney steam vehicle operated by Sir Charles Dance in 1835, but Maudslay was always an internal-combustion-engined vehicle builder and always, as a Continental friend would say, "très solide". After transferring the factory from Coventry to Alcester the company went into the ACV group in 1948 and manufacture — largely a lingering nameplate-only existence — ceased in 1954. In our period of the 'twenties and 'thirties there was for a time a considerable emphasis on passenger models but by 1929 the freight side had advanced to a 10ton

six-wheeled platform lorry with a four-cylinder petrol engine rated at up to 75hp. In that preslump year the company produced a 10 per cent dividend, after which it began to go downhill financially. In 1933 the ingenious Gardner-engined Six-Four lorry was marketed — capable of carrying a six-ton load while coming in the four-ton taxation class — and later the Hobbs automatic gearbox was offered on commercials. Before war broke out the Mogul was the leading freight model and an 80bhp four-cylinder petrol engine was still being offered for it. A complete rejuvenation of output under the energetic O. D. Smith was planned for the 1939 Commercial Show — the show that was cancelled owing to war. There were the rigid six-wheeler, the Maharajah, the Mikado eight-wheeler, and tagging along behind owing to war conditions, the four-wheeled 50cwt chassis for a 6ton load, the Merlin; all were diesel-engined.

Opposite page: The 7-8 ton platform lorry found favour with a Birmingham Brewery.

Below: Ex-War Department 40hp Maudslay of the 1914-18 War. It worked from 1920 for Mr. A. E. Carter (seen driving) who had a Brooke Bond contract for many years.

Bottom: A rigid six-wheel 10-tonner with flat sides.

A 30ft model of Airship R 101 built by employees of LMSR at Coventry for a local carnival on a Maudslay 10-ton lorry.

Below right: A Majestic four-wheeled steering six-wheeler being nonchalantly driven in the Works yard.

Below: A Mogul MkII with special bodywork by Whitson.

Morris Commercial

Brainchild of William Richard Morris, afterwards Lord Nuffield, the Morris Commercial was the first British mass-production load carrier. Panel vans had appeared on Morris car chassis from 1913; the new light lorry came off an assembly line devised in the Wrigley factory at Soho, Birmingham, near where Watt deployed the first extensive production of industrial steam engines. Hollick & Pratt staff devised the body production. Very soon the line was set up in the old Wolseley factory at Adderley Park and challenged the light American freight vehicle in a big way from 1924 onwards. That first one-tonner continued with only small modifications for 15 years, but other products soon came off the Morris-Commercial lines — starting with a double-drive rigid six-wheeler for 30cwt and 2ton loads. The Middleweight Champion was developed as a 30cwt job and the Economy for bulky 2ton loads of low specific gravity — although a capacity to withstand

overloading was admitted if hauliers pressed the point. As the 1930's advanced the products became diversified, including a double-deck bus with detachable engine and front axle, and freight vehicles of 3ton, 3½ton normal control (Leader) and the forward control (Courier) 5-tonner. By 1935 the Leader had stepped up to the 4ton class and a taxi-cab was on the stocks. Towards the end of the decade there appeared the Equi-load series from 25-30cwt to the 4 — 5ton classes, with V-fronted radiator and cab and a forward-mounted engine which maximised the available body space. Variations on wheelbase enabled a chassis particularly suited to tipping work to be supplied and hydraulic tipping gear was offered on the 4 — 5ton short wheelbase model, but hand gear on the 3 — 4tonner. In this size vehicle most makers, including Morris Commercial, stuck to petrol engines at that time. Adderley Park goes on, making the BLMC diesel and petrol 2-tonners today.

Opposite page: A Morris Commercial 2ton tipper being served by an excavator on the site of the new Adderley Park factory for Morris Commercials in the winter of 1935-36.

Below: The original 1ton type preserved and seen in the 1971 Trans-Pennine rally. S. W. Stevens-Stratten

Bottom: The D type 6 by 4 of 1928 with a 2.513 litre four-cylinder petrol engine: one crossed the Kalahari Desert in July, 1928, accompanied by a 1½ton short wheelbase model. As can be seen, tracks are stowed beside the cab and could be fixed on the wheels of the rear bogie for traversing difficult ground. N. J. Painting Collection.

Top left: A new model of the 1ton truck under test in arctic conditions in 1933.

Left: The GPO in 1935 invested in a fleet of streamlined 30cwt vehicles for special air-mail collection, carried out with separate blue pillar boxes.

Above: A 1938 fire tender with bodywork by Jennings of Sandbach stands in front of Kelso Abbey.

Pagefield

Although some of the vehicles offered under this marque were rank ugly, there were a lot of attractive features about the Pagefield and it was a matter of regret to many operators when it left the goods vehicle market after a comparatively short run, although it survived until 1951 in association with municipal equipment. The company, at one time Pagefield Commercial Vehicles Ltd, was associated with Walker Bros (Wigan) Ltd, founded in 1904, of Pagefield Iron Works in that town. A Walker mobile crane of 1930 weighed 18ton all up and was capable of lifting a 6ton load at a 10ft radius. It was designed to meet LMS requirements for transferring containers between road vehicles and railway wagons; the crane and lorry were controlled through Tilling-Stevens petrol-electric gear (with BTH motors) and the whole was mounted on a six-wheeled Pagefield chassis. Road movement was also petrol-electric.

In 1932 a payload of 11ton on a Pagefield Plantagenet six-wheeled chassis was the subject of a test on the Modern Transport Buxton route; the Gardner six-cylinder oil engine and an auxiliary box enabled it to perform over hilly roads in meritorious fashion. The corresponding 6ton four-wheeler was the normal-control Pompian, in which special attention was given to the mountings of the four-cylinder 52hp Gardner engine. In 1933 the Pegasix trailing axle six-wheeler, nominally for 8ton loads, but apparently not distressed by 12ton, was put into production. Another Pagefield speciality in the 'thirties was horse-hauled refuse collectors which could be attached to the diesel-engined unit for a fast motorised run to the dust destructor.

Pagefield Plantagenet six-wheeler at Sparrowpits, near Buxton, while being tested by 'Modern Transport' during 1932.

Below: The Pagefield Flexible 8 to 9ton six-wheeler, made by Walker of Wigan, with its hardly instantaneously detachable semi-trailer.

Bottom left and right: The manufacturer's mobile crane proves useful for the handling of containers; it was said to be capable of lifting a railway wagon from one track and setting it down on another, according to the technical press in 1930.

Peerless

Like the Four Wheel Drive the Peerless was a
1917 wartime importation into this country.
Made by Peerless Motor Company at Cleveland,
Ohio, from about 1905 to 1930, thousands of
them went to France with the American forces.
They were rugged plain petrol jobs, with chain
drive. After the war they were sold off from the
Slough dump, thereby helping to depress the
native manufacturing industry. A reconditioned
Peerless 5-tonner could be bought for £255.
Slough Lorries & Components Ltd, gave place to
Peerless Trading Company and then to Peerless
Lorries Ltd. The Trader was a vehicle assembled
out of available parts and then purpose-built
from 1925 for a decade; some were rumoured
to have been oil-engined. The Tradersix 90 had
an improved distribution of axle weight by
mounting the engine in a fashion popular at the
time forward of the front axle; with pneumatics
on the front wheels and solids on the rear, and
still chain driven, it remained rather on the hard
side for a driver.

*The Peerless Tradersix 90, showing the short chain
drive and the distribution of axle weight, with
pneumatics on the front axle and solids on the rear.*

90

GH BUCKS.

Reo

The Reo chassis was an American importation that was not a product of war but rather of the expansionist riproaring nineteen-twenties when the motor vehicle industry was growing in all directions. Reo Motors Corporation eventually became the Reo Division of the White Motor Company of Lansing, Mich. Here Reo Motors (Britain) Ltd was formed in 1929 and had 30cwt, 2ton and 2½ton chassis on view at the 1929 commercial show. The Gold Crown petrol engine gained a good report for its performance when taken over the Modern Transport test route; a seven-bearing crankshaft was employed and, as with a good many hard-slogging American engines, high torque was produced at low engine speeds. There was a Lanchester vibration damper. The chassis had magazine type lubrication to important points. Another freight vehicle brought over later was a 35cwt with a four-cylinder petrol engine that developed 51bhp. A six-cylinder engine was an alternative and several wheelbases were offered.

The Gold Crown Reo.

Reo Speed Wagon of 1931 at a Historic Commercial
Vehicle Club meeting forty years later.
S. W. Stevens-Stratten.

Tested in the autumn of 1929 on the rough-surfaced
test hills of the 'Modern Transport' Kent and Surrey
route, the Gold Crown Reo gave a good account of
itself. Richard Twelvetrees pre-war vehicle tester sits on
the passenger side of the temporary seat.

Scammell

Scammell tradition goes back much further than is indicated by the formation of Scammell Lorries Ltd in 1922, as it originated with a Spitalfields coachbuilder of Victorian achievement. In those Fashion Street shops the Scammell articulated in 1921 took up an idea of early motor pioneers to get heavier loads and a longer platform, by using a four-wheeled tractor coupled to a two-wheeled semi-trailer to carry a 10ton load without exceeding legal axle weights. The two portions being detachable, one tractor could be used with a variety of semi-trailers, each of which could be made self-supporting at the front end. The present company took over the Watford shops from its predecessor and the board included such heavy haulage pioneers as Ted Rudd (whose business later went into the Tilling group) and Major G. A. Renwick of Manchester — London Steamers. The prototype of 1921 did not get very well recorded, but it had a 63bhp four-cylinder side-valve petrol engine with a compression ratio of 3.75 to 1. The lamps were oil, with candle standby if the oil failed. The Watford production went up to 75bhp and had C A V electric lighting but the firm believed in chain-drive for a trunk service vehicle for many years to come. Very early on (1926) the frameless tanker was introduced. Straight off Scammell tanker owners scored a victory over long-distance milk transporters who relied on the churn. The highly flexible wheel suspension of the Pioneer rigid six-wheeler hit the bullseye with the military and with contractors involved in transport over rough terrain in 1927. During 1932 the final details of the three-wheeled Mechanical Horse were worked out in conjunction with railway companies anxious to rid themselves of horse-hauled cartage, and serious production of a highly successful unit for moving 3 and 6ton semi-trailers began in 1933.

Some early three-wheeled tractors had two-cylinder Jowett opposed piston 7hp car engines, but the Scarab today has Perkins diesel power and there is a four-wheeled version also. Scammell achieved four-wheeled, six-wheeled and eight-wheeled rigid models before the war and some heavy trunk hauliers standardised on these versatile vehicles as far as they were able. Moreover, the company became the largest trailer manufacturer in Europe.

Opposite page: The rugged components of the articulated Scammell made a sturdy four-wheeler for heavy duty work. This one entered Rudd service in 1930.

Bottom: Motive unit of a 100ton machinery carrier of 1927, done up for rally work in the 1960's. S. W. Stevens-Stratten.

Below: A Scammell articulated six-wheeler of 1923, with 80hp petrol engine and 7½ton payload — in this case heavy duty radio equipment. Note the jackshaft is terminated by a brightly polished sprocket wheel interchangeable with one of another size to give different gear ratios for loaded and empty running — more complicated than the two-speed axle or the 10-speed gearbox of today.

Top left: In the thirties the Mechanical Horse
developed for the railways (see Semi-Trailers)
and as a side effect an independent three-wheeled load
carrier was introduced by Scammell.

Left: The apotheosis of the cross-country vehicle for
such work as pipeline laying in the desert was a
Scammell; this one, under test with a load of logs,
appeared in 1932.

Top: Fisher Renwick named their vehicles; Gadwall
was an eight-wheeler for long-distance work delivered
in 1937.

Above: The giant pneumatic tyre seen on a tank wagon
delivered to BP for service in Iran in the mid-thirties.

Semi-Trailers

As will be seen from an illustration the modern idea of the semi-trailer, like so many modern ideas, can be traced back over many years. It seems to be in origin and perfection a British technical concept. With a steerable fore-carriage Burstall's steam coach of 1824 used the principal in reverse and Gurney's steam carriage of a few years later was similar. A commercial vehicle application of tractor and semi-trailer was made by Thornycroft in 1898. The actual builder was the Steam Carriage & Wagon Co Ltd, and the first articulated six-wheeler was notable for winning the premier award in the Liverpool trials of that year. Articulation gave manoeuvrability, even if it posed from the start trials to the unitiated driver upon reversing; it also gave better weight distribution and was used therefore for the 10 and 12-tonners produced by Scammell from 1921 onwards. Although by 1923 the designers had advanced to an articulated bus which received little welcome from police authorities in Britain, a few years passed before Scammell and Karrier both produced, at the instigation of the main-line railway companies, designs for quickly detachable semi-trailers. The motor vehicle firms were incited to conduct research to enable the railways to replace horses on collection and delivery work and John Shearman, Road Motor Engineer of the London Midland & Scottish Railway, was the mainspring of this and also of the experiments which led to the hybrid road and rail vehicle, the Rorailer, built in small numbers about 1930 by Karrier. The freight semi-trailer requirement was that the entire vehicle, of 3 to 6ton capacity, comparable with existing horse-hauled load carriers, should be so easily turned that it could reverse between two railway tracks in the average goods depot. To make the mechanisation economical the trailer had to be detachable so that while it was being loaded or unloaded the motive unit could be handling another trailer on the road. For this purpose both Scammell and Karrier produced three-wheeled power units, but Karrier soon turned to four-wheeled tractors. The Scammell design of quick coupling gear appeared quickly to be favoured by more users than the Karrier system, which we illustrate. The detachable semi-trailer was soon used for a wide range of purposes where its economy could show to advantage. One snag remains for depot clerks — the need to match power unit, coupling gear and trailer.

Opposite page: Grand-daddy of modern semi-trailers seems to be the Thornycroft steam unit of 1898 which gained an award in the famous Liverpool trials.

Below: Prototype Scammell Mechanical Horse undergoing trials in the experimental stage, 1931-32. The Mechanical Horse could turn in a 15ft circle compared with the 23ft plus needed for a horse and cart and the 41ft of a conventional 4ton rigid-framed four-wheeled lorry.

Opposite page: Parallel with the developments at Scammell there were those of Karrier; these two views show the Karrier design of coupling gear uncoupled, with the front end of the trailer supported, and coupled up for haulage.

Above: The Karrier four-wheeled tractor preferred by some users as more stable than a three-wheeler.

Left: A Thornycroft Strenuous tractive unit coupled to a Carrimore quickly detachable semi-trailer.

Above: A Scammell municipal tanker for street washing after poison-gas attacks, hauled by a Mechanical Horse at a demonstration in 1936 and showing that the motor industry was prepared for 1939 even if politicians were not. Topical — Radio Times Hulton Picture Library.

Sentinel

A vast tradition surrounded the Sentinel steam
lorry; it had a neat outline, a good steaming
boiler and an efficient engine and until
legislation cramped its style it was a winner.
When the company turned over to diesel
vehicles it employed the same flair for
originality and efficiency, but it did not get
into quantity production in a postwar market
where there was already a sufficiency of
individual vehicle producers. But triumphing
over all it managed to secure what was probably
the last steam commercial vehicle order placed,
for 250 six-wheeled steamers required by the
Argentine naval authorities in 1950. Alley &
McLellan established the Sentinel in 1906,
removed from Polmadie, Glasgow, to
Shrewsbury in 1918, and there set up a
succession of Sentinel companies which
lasted until 1957 and also made railcars and
locomotives. The works is now a Rolls-Royce
factory. By 1927 Sentinel wagons had
graduated through the Super-Sentinel to a
six-wheeler for a 15ton payload. The platform
was 7ft wide by 20ft long, giving 140sq ft of
area. The four-wheeled rear bogie was designed
for chain drive and to accommodate a 7in
displacement of the axles relatively to one
another in traversing rough sites. The solid fuel
vertical boiler could generate enough steam to
sustain a 90bhp output from the engine. In
1933 the S8 was a 14ton eight-wheeler, the S6
a 10-12ton six-wheeler and the S4 a 6-7ton four-
wheeler. The tare weight rated at about half
the payload. The latest models before the war
included electric speedometer drive, a power
take-off for dynamo, cylinder lubrication and
tyre pump unit, a self-stoking boiler arrangement,
filled through the cab roof, and, of course,
equipment for tipping gear and for keeping tar
hot and other loads cold that come naturally to
a unit with a steam supply on board. Before the
war internal combustion engines and the HSG
gas-producer began to engage Sentinel attention
and Sentinel took the latter over from Gilford
after some successful bus trials in the Highlands.
But, alas, producer gas did not prove popular
with hard-bitten operators and even wartime
necessity did not make it palatable.

A rugged Super-Sentinel tractor supplied in 1930 for timber hauling in Burma, with a wood-burning firebox and powerful winding drum at the back end of the chassis.

Top: Steam power lent itself to refrigeration plant, keeping highly viscous cargoes fluid, and operation of mobile concrete mixing units.

Above: A smartly-finished Sentinel and trailer that helped to build a Portsmouth housing estate and was then transferred to the Isle of Wight.

Right: A Sentinel S4 six-tonner in chassis form, showing steam brake and electric lighting equipment; the acme of steam design by Sentinel Waggon Works (1936) Ltd, of Shrewsbury.

136

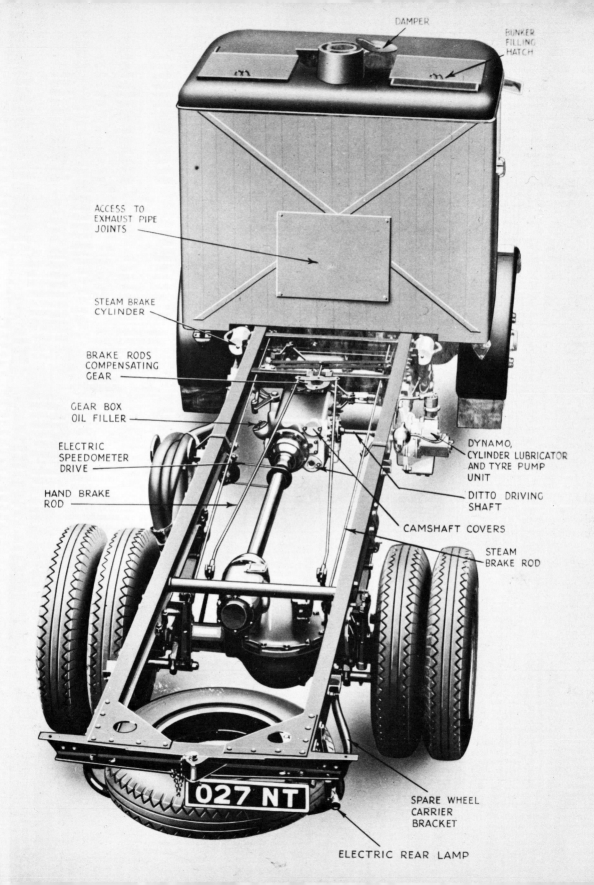

DAMPER

BUNKER FILLING HATCH

ACCESS TO EXHAUST PIPE JOINTS

STEAM BRAKE CYLINDER

BRAKE RODS COMPENSATING GEAR

GEAR BOX OIL FILLER

ELECTRIC SPEEDOMETER DRIVE

HAND BRAKE ROD

DYNAMO, CYLINDER LUBRICATOR AND TYRE PUMP UNIT

DITTO DRIVING SHAFT

CAMSHAFT COVERS

STEAM BRAKE ROD

027 NT

SPARE WHEEL CARRIER BRACKET

ELECTRIC REAR LAMP

Shefflex

To the writer as a student of light railways the Shefflex never impressed itself as a lorry, but only as the motive power and chassis of my friend Colonel Holman Fred Stephens' second generation of back-to-back railbuses that appeared on the West Sussex, Kent & East Sussex and Shropshire & Montgomeryshire Light Railways. But Shefflex Motors Ltd (a name derived from the title of the Sheffield-Simplex Motor Company) was in business as a builder of petrol-engined lorries from 1921 for 12 years and managed to build some extremely average-looking vehicles. In the two-tonners and 2½ton models a four-cylinder petrol engine was offered; it had a power output of 20hp at 1,200rpm and 47bhp at 1,600rpm. There was a ball-bearing-mounted crankshaft which elicited approving comment from the cognoscenti. Cylinders were cast in pairs with fixed heads and valves on the near side, although we believe nothing more than semi-forward control was offered by this maker. A cone clutch was mounted in the cast-steel flywheel and the separate gearbox was driven through a short coupling shaft. An overhead worm drive took the transmission to the rear axle. A single 2½ton exhibit secured a place in the 1929 Olympia show; the 12ft wheelbase chassis and cab tipped the scales at 37cwt and 13cwt was allowed for the tare of the bodywork. The front tyres had 32in by 6in pneumatics and twins of the same dimensions were used on the rear wheels. Electric lighting was supplied.

Apparently rarely photographed, this six-wheeled version of the Shefflex lorry went into the service of a Rutland cement works.

Shelvoke & Drewry

Originality of design went the limit in the drawing offices of Shelvoke & Drewry Ltd at Letchworth. What emerged was a low-loading vehicle with tiny wheels, a straight apron front and a central driving position where the standing driver controlled the vehicle by a pair of handles like the controller of a tramcar. One of these — right-hand-side — steered and the other worked the vertical epicyclic gearbox, which supplied three forward and three reverse speeds. This characteristic brought a moment of grief to my colleague Bill Cornwell, well-known of recent years as a commercial vehicle test engineer of renown, who as a boy in the RAF did some unauthorised driving of an SD Freighter where the usual precaution of blanking off top gear in reverse had not yet been taken after an overhaul. He drove it with panache forwards. When it came to reversing back into the shops he turned round in professional SD driver's style and put his heel on the accelerator, momentarily forgot he was standing back to his original position and that his hands had exchanged functions — and simultaneously changed into reverse top and steered sharply round into a hangar door. A

kindly C O took no further action beyond advising Cornwell to do a welding job on the straightened out door. A miniature trailer to match the power unit had Ackermann steering so that it followed well through narrow spaces. In this unusual chassis the two dry-plate clutches (one for each direction) provided also a transmission brake and sprag gear. The SD Freighter ran on 20in diameter wheels and gave a load line only 1ft 11in off the ground. The normal was a 2-tonner, but there was a reinforced 4ton model first used, we believe, by Guinness in Dublin for moving casks, as it had anti-splash devices round the wheels, then insisted upon by the city authorities there instead of sweeping mud from the streets, The 2-tonner had a 14hp engine, a top speed of 15mph, came in a low taxation category as it weighed less than 2ton and was rated highly for low-speed town work and for jobs where much stopping and starting or shunting were called for. As a result municipal authorities found it ideal for refuse collection and similar duties.

A War Department SD Freighter without cab gets round in a 20ft circle.

Below: The SD Freighter shone in the municipal role between the wars; No 5 of the Epsom & Ewell UDC fleet built in 1934, is here on its way to a rally as an entry by the Worthing Historic Commercial Vehicle Group after renovation and presentation to them by the UDC in 1965; Worthing was one of the towns which saw SD vehicles adapted as the "Tramobus" on its streets. S. W. Stevens-Stratten.

Bottom: An early SD Freighter with small solid rubber tyred wheels. One of the 'tiller' type handles can be seen alongside the drivers central seat.

Singer

From sewing machines to motor cars the name
of Singer has attained widespread fame. The
car business was set up in the first decade of the
century in Coventry but Singer Motors Ltd did
not get round to commercial vehicles until 1928
— and then most of the output was in light vans
based on car models. But between 1929 and
1932 there were a series of lorries of 25cwt,
30cwt, 2ton and 45cwt capacity. The panel vans
on car chassis were discontinued after 1939.
The four-cylinder petrol engine of the 2-tonner
was 90mm bore by 120mm stroke to give a
swept volume of 3053cc. At 3000rpm the
engine turned out something over 57bhp. The
overhead valve rockers were of ingenious design
to reduce wear and the need for adjustment and
the lubrication system, with no loose oilpipes,
showed an appreciation of fundamental design
principles. There was three-point mounting for
the subframe carrying the engine and gearbox
and the engine was insulated from the clutch
and four-speed gearbox unit by rubber buffers.
A specially stiff chassis frame was provided. The
payload of 2ton on that model made an
allowance of 8cwt for bodywork. There was
Marles steering, Luvax foot-operated one-stroke
lubrication of important chassis units and a
floating mounting of the vacuum-servo motor
in the brake rigging. An electric self-starter was
felt by the critics to be an excellent and remark-
worthy refinement.

*A 45cwt Singer lorry (or "Singer Industrial Motor" as
the maker described it) with 500gal tank delivered in
1931.*

143

Star

The Star marque first obtruded itself on my notice as a high-speed passenger vehicle in the service of the Ortona Motor Co Ltd of Cambridge — in the mid-twenties it was good for sustained 40mph running on the Newmarket road. It did not become a numerous freight-carrying vehicle but was highly adaptable to high-speed purposes, such as horsebox operation. From cycles in the nineteenth century (the Star Cycle Company was registered in 1896 to take over from Sherratt & Lisle), it got into motor business in 1904, took the title Star Engineering Co Ltd in 1909, and became the Star Motor Co Ltd in 1928, the year after Guy Motors acquired control. The early commercial adaptations were based on car chassis, and then in the twenties the company produced the Star Flyer and other models,

including tractors. At the 1927 Olympia show the Star freight models were 15cwt, 25cwt and 30cwt vans. A four-cylinder side-by-side valve engine of 3054cc was fitted to the smaller and larger of the trio and an overhead valve job 80mm by 120mm powered the 25cwt unit. The largest body was a 9ft by 5ft 6in by 5ft 10in high van. After 1931 activities were merged in the Guy production.

Produced under the Guy banner, this 1931 Star articulated six-wheeler hauled a Dyson semi-trailer on which was mounted a 1 000cu ft capacity removal van. The motive unit was based on the 50cwt model and the engine had a 23.8hp RAC rating; the outfit could achieve 30mph flat out.

Thornycroft

At the very time of motor vehicle emancipation in 1896 the Thornycroft family had the answer pat. John Isaac Thornycroft (later Sir John) began building steam launches in 1864 and after seven years of experience had achieved the then enormous speed for a river craft of 18 knots. Good steam generation and concentrated engine power went naturally into the 1 ton van and later heavier models. But the path was not easy. There was no high-tensile steel, lifting block chains had to be used for the drive and there were neither solid rubber tyres nor pneumatics for anything bigger than a bicycle. Final handicap — the erecting shop was Sculptor Thomas Thornycroft's Chiswick studio, then occupied by Boadicea in her chariot. Eventually Sir John had to pay for casting the Boadicea group (now on

Westminster Bridge end) himself to get vehicle-building space for the Thornycroft Steam Wagon Co Ltd. Success with compound steam tipping wagons was followed by an award-winning articulated unit in the 1898 Liverpool trials and War Office confidence. Petrol vehicles appeared in 1902 and paraffin-powered ironclads with copper-capped exhaust chimneys two years later. After that road vehicles were developed as a department of John I. Thornycroft & Co Ltd, which was devoted also to shipbuilding. In the period of this album it remained a family concern; hiving off as Transport Equipment (Thornycroft) and eventual transfer first to AEC and then in the BLMC group to Scammell came much later. In the 1914 war the J type covered itself in glory and it was freely adapted in forward-

control bus and lorry forms for some years afterwards. In 1924 the A1 30cwt WD subsidy chassis with unit construction of engine, clutch and gearbox got into flow production at the Basingstoke factory. Rigid six-wheelers and a new 3-tonner appeared two years later and the rigid six developed into the JC 10-tonner and the QC 12-tonner by 1932. The 103bhp petrol engine returned 4.07mpg on a 300 mile 'Modern Transport' test. Type names were discovered to be handy in 1933 and what a profusion was thought up! Four-wheelers included the 2½ton Bulldog, through the Speedy and Strenuous to the 7ton Taurus; the latter had a Thornycroft diesel engine as alternative equipment and the engine compartment was ahead of the front axle. The Handy 2-tonner and Dandy

3-tonner, not to mention the Manly and Beauty, came in the lower load range at this time and the lightweight rigid six-wheeler, the Stag, took a 12ton load for a 7ton tare. A tougher earlier design of rigid six-wheeler, in vogue for tippers, was the 12ton Dreadnought. A lightweight "snout" model (8ton load for a 4ton unladen weight in platform form) was the Trusty of 1934. The following year the Sturdy started a long career as a 4 to 5ton job, soon getting uprated to 6tons. The Dandy was modernised into the 3ton Nippy in 1937 and just before the war the rigid six-wheeler achieved 15ton loads as the Amazon.

Hardly a vehicle manufacturer in the country failed to be proud of a delivery to Carter Paterson and Thornycroft in 1933 was no exception.

Above: Sir John I. Thornycroft stands alongside Steam Van No 1 of 1896; in contrast to the sculptor's Bohemian clothes the driver has elected to wear full morning dress.

Above right: By 1903 the driver of the Thornycroft steam lift van in Whiteley's service was more appropriately dressed in dungarees.

Right: A Thornycroft J-type of 1920, supplied in the early days of a famous tanker fleet when petrol was still delivered in cans; the body on this one could carry 500 two-gallon tins.

Top: A 2½ton petrol vehicle (unladen weight 2ton 8cwt) engaged in marmalade delivery in 1910.

Above: The snout type Trusty developed into a six-wheeler for an overseas customer.

Top: In Palace Yard: Prominent members of the
House of Commons stand by a Thornycroft touring
cinema in 1934 on handing over a Conservative film
that was to tour the country.
Left to right: Stanley Baldwin, Sir John Simon and
J. Ramsay MacDonald.

Above: A wartime delivery of a Sturdy.

151

Trojan

About the same time that Herbert Austin had his inspiration to design the Austin Seven, handsome little money-maker, L. H. Hounsfield designed a weirdly ugly little beast of 10hp which helped the great Leyland company out of the difficulties of the first of the between-the-wars slumps. In 1924 the Trojan came out with solid tyres, long cantilever springs which smoothed out their dire effects, chassisless characteristics, a 10hp four-cylinder two-stroke petrol engine (only seven moving parts!), pedal-operated epicyclic gearbox, austere body styling and in

one series — to the delight of the connoisseur of the extraordinary — pressed steel wheels ribbed with imitation spokes just like cheap toy tinplate mail vans. The commercial version was soon snapped up for 5cwt loads and Brooke Bond Tea placed large orders. The thin solid-tyred wheels could get caught in the tramlines, but Brooke Bond did not subscribe to the music hall joke that a shortage of tea was caused by all their vans having to go to the tram depot to get taken off the track. Leyland took up manufacture and at one time the Kingston works turned out

85 a week. The association ended in 1928, after which Trojan Ltd did its own production on a smaller scale at Croydon and sent forth a range of pneumatic-tyred vehicles, while the Kingston Works went on to the Leyland Cub. The 1929 Trojan output included 7cwt and (with bigger springs) 10cwt four-wheeled models and a six-wheeled 15cwt vehicle. Eight years later the range was similar with a 12cwt Senior four-wheeled van of 160cu ft capacity, on a forward control 8ft wheelbase chassis with Bendix-Cowdray brakes. The two-stroke four-cylinder 12bhp at 1250rpm water-cooled engine, with 2½in bore and 4⅝in stroke and two-speed and reverse epicyclic gearbox still dominated the specification and nearly £½ a million of commercial orders were reported to be on the books at that time.

A Trojan with auxiliary gearbox and track to spread load and torque on the rear bogie climbs a 1 in 2 gradient on the South Downs in 1929.

A 1934 Trojan Van, typical of the once popular make, this one, now happily preserved, growls along the Brighton road with the characteristic noise from its chain drive. S. W. Stevens-Stratten

Pneumatic-tyred Trojan of the 1930's restored for rallies. S. W. Stevens-Stratten

Unipower

Large industrial tractors and forestry machines with four-wheel drive, special power takeoff equipment and winches have been built since 1937 by Universal Power Drives Ltd of Perivale, Middlesex, under the name of Unipower. Over a year after the debut at the Earls Court show we took a Unipower tractor round the 'Modern Transport' test route. It had a Hercules six-cylinder petrol engine which produced 85bhp at 2800rpm; drive was taken through a 13in diameter single dry plate clutch, a five-speed primary gearbox and a two-speed auxiliary box, thus giving 10 forward speeds and two reverse. The four-wheel drive was conveyed by balanced tubular propeller shafts with Hardy Spicer needle roller bearings to the differentials. The front wheels then were driven through Rzeppa high-angle constant velocity joints, an arrangement found very satisfactory for transmission through a wide angle of steering lock and for remaining troublefree under stress. Brakes were Girling wedge-operated equipment in 16in drums, actuated by a Clayton Dewandre vacuum-servo. The unit tested was operating for the Unilever group, hauling a Crane eight-wheeled (four sets of two in trunnion mountings) vacuum-braked trailer. A 14ton load was picked up and the entire outfit was accelerated to its then legal limit of 20mph in 40sec using the auxiliary low gear. But in the high gear it achieved the legal top speed in 32sec. The respective top speeds were 25 and 45mph. On a 12mile trip the petrol consumption with this load was 5mpg. The steering was so accurate that it was possible to traverse the sharply curving narrow carriageway of the old Blackwall Tunnel (where buses had special thick-walled tyres) without rubbing the kerbs.

A Unipower tractor working for the London Oil & Cake Mills in 1938.

Vulcan

One of the famous names in commercial vehicles manufacture that has disappeared is Vulcan. There was a steam traction engine builder in Beccles, Suffolk, from 1884 onwards; a company set up to build steam and petrol lorries and petrol buses was Vulcam Motor Manufacturing & Engineering Co Ltd of 1903 and became Vulcan Motor & Engineering Co Ltd three years later. At the end of the thirties the company was merged in Tilling-Stevens Motors Ltd and after the takeover by the Rootes group Vulcan had ceased as a separate make by 1953. Before the Tilling-Stevens period at Maidstone, where the Vulcan was produced in a remarkable multi-storey factory at one time devoted to electric motors, Vulcan was associated with Crossens near Southport. From there a considerable array of small lorries and an occasional double-deck psv appeared in the 'twenties and 'thirties, but financial success eluded the company. Nevertheless the 3ton low-loading Runabout lorry with 20in wheels (a rival to the SD) and the 4 to 5ton cross-country six-wheeler for the War Office were notable vehicles of the mid-twenties. At the 1937 Earls Court Exhibition there were up from Southport no fewer than six freight models; a 2½ton forward control Luton van; a 5ton forward control tipping lorry, with Gardner 4LK diesel engine, a cattle wagon, a 35cwt normal control lorry, and a 5-tonner in chassis and complete forms. Marles-Weller steering gear and Lockheed hydraulic actuation (assisted by Vacuum servo) of Vulcan four-wheel brakes were specified on the 5ton tipper, which had Edbro 3E twin-ram tipping gear, mounted behind the cab. The licensing weight of this unit was less than 3ton.

An early petrol-engined Vulcan lovingly restored.

Top: A Vulcan Runabout 3ton low-loader supplied to Peterborough Co-operative Society in the 1920's. This handy unit, with platform 4in above standard to meet the user's requirements had a turning circle of 32ft.

Above: A 5ton dropside lorry supplied for brick haulage in 1937.